MODERN ASIAN LIVING

MODERN ASIAN LIVING

Wongvipa Devahastin na Ayudhya and Sakul Intakul
Text: Kim Inglis
Photography: Masano Kawana

PERIPLUS

Published by Periplus Editions (HK) Ltd

Copyright © 2005 Periplus Editions (HK) Ltd

ISBN 0-7946-0291-6
Printed in Singapore
Edited by: Kim Inglis
Design: Holger Jacobs and Gennett Agbenu at Mind Design

Distributed by:
North America
Tuttle Publishing, 364 Innovation Drive,
North Clarendon, VT 05759-9436, USA
Tel (802) 773 8930; fax (802) 773 6993

Asia Pacific
Berkeley Books Pte Ltd,
130 Joo Seng Road, #06-01/03,
Singapore 368357
Tel (65) 6280 3320; fax (65) 6280 6290

Japan and Korea
Tuttle Publishing, RK Building, 2nd Floor,
2-13-10 Shimo-Meguro, Meguro-Ku,
Tokyo 153, Japan
Tel (813) 5437 0171; fax (813) 5437 0755

Half-title page
Reproduction of Charles Rennie Mackintosh designed Ladder Back chair in the pristine confines of architect Khun Tinakorn Rujinarong's house.

Title page
Hallway in the home of Khun Korakot Srivikorn which was designed by Duangrit Bunnag, one of Thailand's premier young architects.

Right
Philippe Starck chair aside three pots with pointed agave leaves in the gallery-style home of Tinakorn Rujinarong.

Opposite
DWP Cityspace designed the offices of Hutchison Wireless with panache: primary colors and bold graphics characterize the non-office style spaces.

CONTENTS

THE NEW ASIAN DESIGN

When international design luminaries such as Christian Liaigre or Christina Ong set up shop in a city, it's not an everyday occurrence. After all, these are big international names: Ong's Como Hotels is readily recognized as an icon for hip hostelries; and with clients like Calvin Klein, Karl Lagerfeld and Kenzo to name a few, Liaigre's sleek, luxe furniture and interior design style is now a global brand. So when they chose Bangkok for the new Metropolitan hotel and furniture showroom Hylé, design mavens worldwide stood up and took note.

One thing this cool hotelier and hot designer have in common is an up-to-the-minute aesthetic that combines the best elements of East and West. In *Modern Asian Living*, we showcase a number of spaces — residential, commercial and recreational — that embrace the spirit of modernity that imbues Ong and Liaigre's work. Like their designs, these mostly metropolitan spaces epitomize the modern exotic, yet they rely to a certain extent on tradition. Pan-Asian craftsmanship, motifs and cultural references are mixed with new materials, shapes and forms. Many were created by upcoming names in Bangkok's design scene.

Take Duangrit Bunnag, for example. Lauded as an important "voice" in Thai architectural circles, his work is more Corbusien than Thai. There's a sophisticated simplicity and restraint in his clean-lined projects, yet he insists they are Asian at heart. "Asian architecture isn't about romantic or rustic spaces," he explains. "There also isn't really a set style. What it is about is a philosophy of simplicity — but this isn't even minimal, just sufficient." Check out the house he designed for friends on page 196.

In fact, when we look closely at the homes in the book, it becomes clear that many are rooted in Asian tradition. The shop-house apartment conversion featured on pages 34–39, though no longer narrow and thin because walls have been knocked down, still follows the customary configuration overlooking an internal courtyard. This is true, also, of the recently constructed city-center housing development, the Lofts Sathorn (pages 136–143). DWP Cityspace principal Scott Whittaker explains the concept: "I wanted to create a new model for inner city housing that is spacious and light with internal and external spaces," he says. "But even though the design is contemporary and wasn't inspired by traditional Thai forms, there are many parallels with the shophouse model."

Acclaimed furniture, product and interior designer Ou Baholyodhin sees this Asian influence everywhere. Even though he is now based in London, he travels to Thailand frequently and incorporates an oriental aesthetic from his home country in much of his work. He says that Thais are not immune to the media power of Western giants in fashion, art and interiors, but the best of Thai design keeps true to its roots. "We are a proud nation," he notes, "and however much we are influenced by the West, our designers still strive to maintain their unique culture and tradition."

This is clearly apparent in many of the interiors in this book. Utilizing Asian-designed and made furniture and furnishings, state-of-the-art lighting systems and the work of local artists and sculptors, the enormous variety in interior décor is impressive. Be it a knock-your-socks-off al fresco bar and restaurant in the sky, a small apartment or high-tech office, individuality and imagination are rampant. The growth of innovative, high-quality Asian furniture designers, as well as soft furnishing, tableware and interior design companies is extraordinary. We give a complete listing of stockists at the end of the book.

Rocky Hizon of Budji Living (a home concept "store" featured on pages 50–55) sees some ground breaking trends in the global furniture market. "In the past we would see Western furniture and interior design ideas permeating Asia," she says, "but today there is a shift towards Asian furniture and design ideas in the West. People there are looking at the huge talent we have here. More innovative designers are using natural materials that are beaten, pressed, polished, woven and stained — and the result is more high-end furniture." In the showroom of Budji Living, there are examples of furniture pieces by top designers in the Philippines that have wowed the crowds at Milan's furniture fairs — and are now being exported all over the world.

A living room in central Bangkok decked out with Christian Liaigre-designed furniture from Hylé, the designer's shop that opened in Bangkok in 2004. The low-level coffee-table and chairs in dark wood display the sober aesthetic the designer is so famed for. The large oil on canvas on right (*Untitled* 2002) is by Taiwijit Peungkasemsomboon and Somyot Hananuntasuk; an experiment in collaborative art, each artist had to maintain his own identity as well as blending with the other.

The same is true of leather designers and manufacturers Paragon International. Their world-class lines retail in many an upscale department store, and you'll see their signature pieces in all the European capitals as well as New York, Sydney, Tokyo and Singapore. "Our aim is to produce exclusive products that have a timeless elegance," says partner Vichien Chansevikul, "these range from the custom designed to the hip and trendy, as well as the classic."

One notable improvement in all these furniture companies is in the quality; standards, especially in the finishing, are now very high. That, combined with innovative forms and enticing prices, has contributed in no small part to their success. Another interesting development is the growth of the concept store or one-stop shopping mall. Bangkok's Gaysorn Plaza and Discovery Center are established venues for home furnishers. Featuring a plethora of home décor outlets in a foward-looking, light and airy mall, we've singled out Vihayas (pages 86–91) as the cream of the crop. A multi-disciplinary store, it is the first choice for many: here you can browse for clothes or candles, tableware or knick-knacks — or simply chill in the boho-chic bar. Cool tunes and eclectic reading material make your retail experience therapeutic.

The H1 complex (pages 166–177) has taken the lifestyle concept one step further. Billing itself as an "escape," it comprises a number of sleek, contemporary, low-rise buildings linked by courtyards and innovative landscaping. You can eat, shop, browse, drink, or simply indulge in a spot of people watching: all the outlets are a treat for the eye, and design-conscious folk love both the trendy vibe and the products on sale. It's a top example of how creative collaboration can produce something truly unique.

Unique, too, are the floral arrangements and installations in the book. The work of Thailand's renowned flower maestro Khun Sakul Intakul, they cover the spectrum from dramatic to demure, sculptural and unconventional to poignant and petite. Always appropriate to site and setting, they're imaginative fodder for the wannabe florist. Many are easy to recreate at home, and all are

interchangeable with both tropical and temperate leaves and blooms. They accompany the inspired styling of Khun Wongvipa Davahastin na Ayudhya admirably. "In this book the flower arrangements were created as a means of conveying our perceptions of the atmosphere and mood of each location," Khun Sakul explains. "Light, color, style, the selection of furniture and decorative items and the texture and form of each interior are all important elements when formulating an arrangement."

Modern Asian Living is both an up-to-date directory of the region's top product and interior designers, architects and landscape architects, and a showcase of inspirational ideas. It covers a wide spectrum of pan-Asian design: The first chapter 'Tranquil Living' looks at what Rocky Hizon calls spaces "where nothing clouds the mind...[that are] pressure-relieving, Zen, with greater *chi* and a feeling of lightness and transparency"; 'Drama' is a collection of highly dramatic, for the most part colorful, interiors; while 'Light & Space' deals with the way homes in the tropics integrate their living spaces with the outdoors, with breezy, beautiful results. The three chapters are very different in atmosphere and ambience, but all have one thing in common — a commitment to excellence and a desire to break boundaries.

As Ou Baholyodhin concludes: "Good design must come from a profound understanding; it's hard to explain, but you know what's good when you see it." Read through the following pages, enjoy the visuals — and see what he means.

The living room in leather designers and manufacturers Vichien Chansevikul and Michael Palmer's converted shophouse home is full of light and space. The poufs are from their company Leather Paragon, while the sofa was custom-designed by the pair for the corner. Inset alcoves displaying choice mementoes echo the shape of the huge panelled floor-to-ceiling window.

TRANQUIL LIVING

A calm, restful environment soothes, restores and rejuvenates. Natural, organic materials (inside and out), quality artworks and a spirited outlook combine with airy, open spaces to produce a simple, uncluttered look. Attention to detail, good flow of *qi* and cool colors are paramount. The pan-Asian aesthetic here is pared down: results are more Zen den than Oriental opulent, and impressively restful.

BAAN SUAN SANGHOB

Right
The exterior of the house as
seen from the side in its
jungle setting. According to
the architect, steel structures
can be slimmer than heavier
concrete ones, thus enhanc-
ing the feeling of light and
space within.

Below
The house took about six
months to design and two
years to complete with the
ground-breaking ceremony
taking place on the 19th day
of the 9th month of the year
1999 at 9:00 am. This view
shows the wooden deck that
leads into the front door
of the house. Note the door
handle — a propeller from
a plane.

Baan Suan Sanghob or the "Tranquil Garden House" is the home of Prabhakorn Vadanyakul, managing director of Architects 49, one of Thailand's premier architectural practices. Specializing in forward-looking works, A49 is celebrated for its innovative approach to architecture, design and landscape design. Appropriately enough, the house was designed by Khun Prabhakorn and built by A49 staff.

Set on the outskirts of the city on a plot of land planted by Khun Prabhakorn's father with seeds collected from around the country, the three-story house showcases mature trees at every turn. Built predominantly from steel and glass, it is light, airy and cool; it can either be fully air-conditioned, or parts of its structure may be opened up to encourage cross ventilation. Thus, there are minimal boundaries separating it from its lush, untamed natural environment.

"I wanted to prove that modern construction materials are not at odds with nature," explains the architect, "I also wanted to show that you don't need solid walls to separate the inhabitants from their surroundings." Hence, Khun Prabhakorn and his wife experience a type of indoor/outdoor tropical living style that perfectly suits site, setting, context and climate.

An avid aviation fan (both he and his wife are pilots), Khun Prabhakorn brings his lifelong obsession with the mechanical into the design of the house. Stainless steel tension cables, doors in the shape of plane doors, a long custom-designed bench on the terrace in the shape of a plane wing, steel mesh walkways and exposed pipes combine with strictly utilitarian materials to give an industrial feel. This is softened and humanized by the plethora of vegetation all around — as well as by the pool and use of wood.

In keeping with the architecture, aggressively sculptural Mario Botta furniture is used sparingly throughout. Made from steel, perforated sheet metal and polyurethane, its rigid forms complement both the architecture and the owner's collection of mechanical toys. However, it needs to be stressed that this glass-and-steel house never for a minute seems out of place in its jungle situation. Rather, by inviting in light, air, the breeze and the trees, it becomes a modern take on a traditional tree house.

Above

The expansive dining room looks out on to a downstairs deck with hammock and loungers facing a pool that seems to melt into the trees beyond. Decorative cabbages in glass vases from anyroom nestle in a pot pourri from Siamrak on the black galvanized steel table; the pot pourri of seeds was chosen because Khun Prabhakorn's father planted the garden with seeds collected from all over Thailand.

Left

The open-plan living room features polished sandstone floors, unadorned walls, simple furniture and floor-to-ceiling glass windows. Khun Prabhakorn says that these glass "walls" act only as space indicators — and give views on to the garden from all sides.

Left
An open wood staircase
leads up to the first floor.
The treads were designed
to replicate the flaps on
a plane wing.

The upstairs deck leads off the master bedroom — and affords superb views of the forest. Some of the trees are as high as a ten-story building, and even though the plot is surrounded by huge shopping malls, shophouses, highways and traffic, you'd never know it once you are ensconced in this private arboretum.

Far left
A metal and shiny canvas lounger on the top deck.

Left
At the front entrance Khun Prabhakorn installed a modern take on the traditional foot bath used to wash the feet before entering a Thai home. Made from one slab of granite, it is situated just before the front entrance landing.

Opposite
The long lap pool as soon from above. Tiled in aquamarine, it is surrounded by mature trees and overgrown heliconias.

All the bathrooms are fitted out with plane doors on sliding wheels, industrial-style fittings and exposed concrete walls. The downstairs cloakroom is quite utilitarian, the only decoration taking the form of steel "wheels" on the sink.

Left
A shower cubicle showcases exposed water pipes, a metal showerhead, and unconcealed nuts and bolts. It isn't really "boarding house basic," but comes close for sure!

Right and far right
Part of the owner's collection of mechanical toys.

Opposite
The master bedroom sports polished cement walls, with factory-style light switches. Light wood parquet flooring and a low-level platform bed with fluffy white duvet soften the hard architectural edges.

ARTFUL LIVING

The home of Ek-Annong Phanachet and Carlos Manalac is elegant, clean-lined and serene. Originally designed for a Thai businessman with a Japanese wife by noted French interiors and furniture designer Christian Liaigre, it retains design stamps from its first owners and its present ones. Although vastly different in background, both sets of owners have a love of art — and this goes some way to explaining the large gallery-style spaces within. It also explains the "real" art gallery next door (see right, below).

High ceilings, floor-to-ceiling glass windows, spacious rooms and floor track up lighting are statement-making aspects of this well-designed house. Comprising about 800 square meters (8,600 sq ft) in total, it has a pan-Asian feel that is both contemplative and contemporary. Apt then to find understated Christian Liaigre-designed furniture — in neutral tones — laid out with symmetry and simplicity in the perfectly proportioned living room. Here, massive glass windows are covered by three layers of amber-colored Jim Thompson unlined silk curtains; these contain the harsh glare of the Bangkok sun, but allow for glimpses of garden behind. They also allow for a slightly diffused light within.

Christian Liaigre is perhaps best known as the interior designer of New York's Mercer Hotel, but confesses to prefer smaller, residential projects. His combination of exotic dark woods and luxurious fabrics is illustrated in the dining room of this house, where a slatted wooden screen door opens to reveal a calm, formal dining room. Three silk lampshades above the dining table echo the color of the curtains, while the heaviness of dark furniture is alleviated by light parquet flooring. The room is calm, formal and understated.

Leading off the dining room is a more informal, relaxed family room, where Noon the pug curls up for a snooze and Ek-Annong and her husband take time out from their busy schedules. Natural furniture in modern designs by award-winning young Thai designers give the room a funky feel. The organic factor is furthered upstairs where a simple, meditative swimming pool shares space with the three bedrooms on the second floor. Here, more art pieces in wood and ceramic are displayed in peaceful poolside surrounds.

Left
The family den (foreground) has wooden pivoting doors that open up fully to give views into the formal dining room — and beyond into the tree-lined street.

Below
Situated adjacent Ek-Anong Phanachet's residence at 100 Soi Tonson is 100 Tonson Gallery. It has the lofty aim of making a vital contribution to the visual arts culture in Thailand. The gallery organizes a minimum of four to five exhibitions annually, including a curated exhibition; space is dedicated mostly to contemporary Thai art. Built from concrete, the gallery is a box-like structure with high ceilings and plenty of natural light mainly procured from skylights. For more details visit www.100tonsongallery.com.

Above and right
The kitchen is an assured combo of wood and stainless steel fittings. The solid table and bench by Saiyart Sema-Ngern is an artwork in itself. All stonewares on the table and counter are by Eakrit Praditsuwana for E.G.G Enterprise.

Opposite
A suitably opulent dining atmosphere is achieved with fine tableware and napkins that match the drapes and lampshades. Taking its inspiration from a Japanese ikebana device called a *kenzan*, whereby lead blocks are spiked with brass nails, delicate blue iris are secured in galvanized iron square trays along the center of the table. Their cool blue hues contrast beautifully with the ocher shades above.

The family room features rattan, *yan lipao* (a weed from the south of Thailand) and water hyacinth furniture as well as tactile rugs in organics from a variety of artisans, artists and interior shops in Bangkok.

Clockwise from top left
Low-level lounging chair in rattan with metal legs by Udom Udomsrianan of Planet 2001. The chair was an award winner at the Milan Furniture Fair in 2003. The water hyacinth rug in neutral tones is from Ayodhaya. Rustic chair designed and constructed by Thai National Artist Saiyart Sema-Ngern sits behind a handmade rug by Rapee Leelasiri, chief designer at Graph-TEX Studio. Khun Rapee is a multiple award winner for her stylish rugs in natural fibers. Central rattan and glass Threesome coffee table by Udom Udomsrianan.

Crystal wine glasses and champagne flutes with hand-crafted silver stems with gems were designed by Tam Devakul of T Positif. The handmade hammered-work cutlery and under plates are from Niwat at Gaysorn Plaza. The glasses' elegant lines and clean, modern shapes complement the long central flower arrangement by Khun Sakul where tubes of banana leaves form a base structure and green cattelya are housed in a long, slim acrylic vase from Cocoon. Christian Liagre organic-style wood side table. An installation on the stairs by Sakul Intakul features white cattleya hanging in light porcelain "senna" vessels created by the designer. Sinuous curving detail of low-level *yan lipao* loveseat by Suwan Kongkhunthian at Yokatha with brown raw silk cushions. A single bright red-and-yellow cattleya sits in a "tri-pod" bronze flower vessel designed by Sakul Intakul. Close-up detail of Fringe Design pouf by M.L. Pawinee Santisiri at Ayodhaya.

Right
Khun Ek-Annong's house is a veritable treasure trove of art. Adjacent the stairs is displayed a large blue-toned painting "Cyber Baby" (2003) by British artist, Andrew Stahl. It is one of a collection he painted whilst he was Artist in Residence at Silpakorn University in the summer of 2003. On left on the stairs is the hanging white cattelya arrangement seen on previous page.

Left
Beneath the painting entitled "A Day in the Life" by Chatchai Puipia is a large black leather pouf called the Black Spaceship by Udom Udomsrianan for Planet 2001. Wooden stools by Christian Liaigre.

Far left
On the far wall is a painting called "2002–20" by Somyot Hananuntasuk; the two black stools on right were bought locally.

Left
Above a dark stained wooden stool by Christian Liaigre is a painting entitled "Guitar" by acclaimed Spanish painter Ginés Serrán-Pagan. A mixed technique on canvas piece, it was painted in 2003.

A bench fashioned from
railway sleepers designed
and crafted by Saiyart Sema-
Ngern and Thailand National
Artist Nithi Sathapitanonda.

"Prai 1" (100 x 70 x 35 cm) a
ceramic stoneware sculpture
by Amornthep Mahamart
(2003). *Prai* translates from
the Thai as "water bubbles"
and the sculpture floats if
put in water.

Concrete girders frame
downtown views from the
third-floor poolside; at the
far end is a bench fashioned
from an old boat, also by
Saiyart Sema-Ngern and
Nithi Sathapitanonda.
"The benches are intended
as functional art," says Khun
Ek-Annong, "and are great
showpieces for the contemporary art scene in Thailand
today."

SHOPHOUSE CHIC

The shophouse model in Asia is a compact one, but is often criticized by modern city-dwellers for being too long and thin. This apartment, created by taking the top floor of three shophouses and knocking down the dividing walls between, does away with the long/thin configuration and comes up with a spacious alternative. The owner Vichien Chansevikul and his partner Michael Palmer design, manufacture and export leather home décor items and furniture in the first three floors of the shophouses below — and live in splendor above.

Access is from the third storey of one of the outer shophouses. The central focus of the apartment is an enormous living room with open-plan dining area and kitchen. Clean, airy and light, it was designed by the owners with a little help from an architect friend. A wonderful, polished timber floor in *teng* wood was laid during construction, and it adds a warm sheen to the contemporary styled room. The adjacent dining area, cleverly divided off from the kitchen by a false wall that houses bottles of wine, is a little small, but ideal for entertaining in a relaxed, casual manner. Because there are no views to speak of, the rooms all look inward over a central courtyard. It's from here that light pours into the interior — from huge wall-to-wall aluminum-and-glass windows.

Unsurprisingly, furniture is imprinted with the flair and style of the two partners. The cream-colored, l-shaped sofa suite was designed by the pair, but made in a friend's factory that specializes in padded furniture. It is complemented by plain and woven leather poufs in turquoise and dark brown. Of note are the cushions made from leather embossed with a woven rattan effect. Elsewhere in the room are textural, beautifully finished pieces from the couple's leather lines: plant stands in faux-croc leather, a nest of tables in wood and woven rattan, a console in wood-and-leather — and more.

Overall, the apartment illustrates how shophouses may be re-designed and re-configured for a more modern feel, all the while retaining the character of the original. The timber floors and internal courtyard are reminiscent of the past, while the airy spaces and modern furniture look forward to the future. And because of its situation, the pair has no excuse for being late for work!

Left
Floor-to-ceiling paneled and tinted windows run the length of the generously proportioned living room. Furnished simply in tones of beige and brown, the custom-crafted corner sofa with bolsters encourages relaxed lounging. A rectangular box in tan leather in the foreground is sized for magazine storage, while two different styles of pouf and a cylindrical, layered lamp (all from Leather Paragon) are featured. Reed mace secured with a leather band makes for a minimalist arrangement in a mock croc leather vase, also from Leather Paragon.

Below
Beneath a wall with inset display niches sits a console with three drawers designed to look like a traditional Chinese console. It is from Leather Paragon's most recent collection and was shown at the B.I.G. Fair in April 2004 for the first time. It is made from rubber wood and the cow leather used has a small crocodile imprint in dark brown.

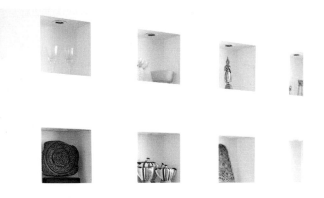

Left
A two-toned console made from rubber wood and topped with lizard-imprinted cow leather is placed in the master bedroom across from the courtyard. Beneath is a wooden trunk with a leather lid, while on top are two identical vases housig red amaryllis lilies.

This page,
clockwise from top left
Detailed workmanship in different leather toned checks on a side table. Three-drawer console with wine or champagne bucket featuring a stainless steel inner and a leather outer with handles. Close-up detailing of the dining area metallic chandelier. Close-up of a ring-leg nest of tables where frames are in rubber wood and the tops are made from woven rattan leather (it comes in three colors); above is a ceramic pot from Chiang Mai. Leather handles on wood. Reed mace secured with a leather band in a mock croc leather vase. All items from Leather Paragon.

COOL BLUE

Right

An appealing mix of cool blues and natural organics: Udom Udomsrianan, whose works have been exhibited at the George Pompidou Center in Paris and at Japan's HARA Contemporary Museum, is known for his experimental furniture. This screen and chair are both decorative and utilitarian. The Nitti Wathuya blue-toned painting goes well with a Chinese carpet bought in Taipei.

Below

The apartment has panoramic views over the marina where the owner s have a mooring for their converted Thai fishing boat (their other craft, a yacht designed by Ed Tuttle comprises part of the Aman fleet at Amanpuri). Here we see the view from the bedroom window and a table constructed from one piece of free form wood in front of it.

The marine-inspired palette of this Pattaya apartment came about more by accident than design — but makes for a fitting décor scheme as it overlooks the marina. Furthermore, it is owned by a couple who love the sea, own a luxurious yacht, and like to sail whenever possible. Apt then, that blue is the dominant color.

That, along with the liberal use of organics and unusual Eastern art, makes this a unique space. The French Oriental Art dealer owner, Jean-Michel Beurdeley, and his Thai wife Patsy divide their time between Paris and Bangkok — and use the condo on weekends when they want to go sailing. The Beurdeley's love of art and the sea is evident at every turn.

The first thing one sees on entering the apartment is a custom-designed screen made from woven rattan slotted into a nearly square, dark wood frame. Hand-crafted by Udom Udomsrianan, it prevents people outside from looking in when the entrance door is open, and also has good feng shui. "We were attracted by the simplicity of the natural material and the modernity of rattan and water hyacinth furniture from Udom," explains Jean-Michel, "His pieces look like modern sculptures."

Once round the screen, a large open-plan reception room with dining room at left is revealed. Here floor-to-ceiling windows bring in light and marina views, and more furniture including a glass-and-water hyacinth coffee table by Udom as well as a custom-crafted sofa by Sompong Panich. A Japanese screen featuring two lions is the dominant decorative feature.

Jean-Michel decided to do without a third bedroom, and knocked through the wall to introduce an adjoining dining room. Here an Italian dining table and chairs is offset by a beautiful plaster relief from an original mould from a wall in Angkor Wat. Conversely, adding a more modernist touch, is a contemporary painting by Professor Precha Thaothong in tones of grey. "We hope we've achieved something original here," says Jean-Michel. "We've tried to avoid the usual by mixing some Thai modern paintings with old Chinese rocks, sculptures and other objects; it is fun to mix modern and old."

The airy, open living room is cool and inviting, with an unpretentious and welcoming atmosphere that is subtly accentuated by the priceless art on display. On the Udom Udomsrianan central low-level glass and water hyacinth coffee table sits an iron dancing figure crafted by Jean-Michel. Adjacent the Japanese screen (*see overleaf*) is a 19th-century Chinese natural stone "sculpture" on a carved stand. Chinese scholars used to collect these *zen* or *chan* pieces for meditative purposes; the rock may symbolize water.

Above
A Japanese screen depicting two lions hangs above the in-built sofa in the living room. In the north east, during an annual ceremony, monks distribute tracts to the populace; they've been used here to cover two bolsters.

Far left
A lady's slipper orchid is deftly arranged in a pandanus leaf which in turn is housed within a glass vase.

Left
Clay figurine of Chinese god, 18th century.

Right
Much of the ironwork in the apartment was fashioned by Jean-Michel into a number of abstract sculptures, seen here decorating the restful dining room. Pride of place, however, goes to a plaster relief from an original mould from a wall in Angkor Wat; it was used for the colonial exhibition in Paris in 1920.

THAI-STYLE MODERN

This compact, open-plan apartment is a good example of how minimal space can be used to dramatic effect. The home of Wisit Jivakul, the managing director of a Bangkok architecture firm, Le Motif, it is extremely well planned and executed to gain maximum benefit from a small floor area.

Many people, especially in urban centers in Asia, live in apartments that are tiny by international standards. High real estate prices, lack of land and large populations have brought this about, most notably in cities like Tokyo and Hong Kong. In the case of Khun Wisit who lives alone, his small unit was bought many years ago but a recent renovation has opened it up significantly. Removing many of the poky apartment's walls produced a large living room with an open kitchen corner, a dining corner, a study area and a terrace radiating around this central core. A bathroom and bedroom with walk-in closet completes the bachelor pad nicely.

Because the apartment consists, in effect, of one expansive, open space, it appears larger than it is in reality. This is accentuated by the use of different materials introducing the small annexes: a polished aqua-green flossed glass wall cleverly lit to glow for the dining area, a wooden panel for the study platform, and Venetian blinds for access to the terrace. Also the fact that the space has been left fairly uncluttered further contributes to the feeling of light and space; the apartment is almost ornament free.

Furniture has been chosen with care. A centrally placed low table (*ma-kha*) and Thai triangular cushions are left stacked together and may be moved by guests as they please. Khun Wisit designed the dining table himself and has bought a very good quality copy of Mies van de Rohe's Barcelona chair for his lounging corner. In the bedroom a mattress on a natural fiber rug and a sandstone floor in the bathroom continue the simplistic theme.

"I tried to adapt Thai living with a contemporary and minimalist style," explains Khun Wisit. "The living room with low seating, the platform area, the bed on the floor — are all examples of this. For me, the living room is the heart of the apartment and the small open niches around it form a functional whole."

Left
A low desk with laptop, concealed television in a cupboard and elegant standing lamp from Panta are packed into the small study corner backed with wood.

Below
The open-plan kitchen is separated from the other parts of the apartment by a chest-high dividing wall. Built-in glass-fronted cupboards sit above, while the utilities are housed beneath the counter top below an exposed brick wall. At center is a slightly sinister, masculine bat flower in a stainless steel container from anyroom; it sits on a wooden shelf that juts out from the dividing wall. Adjacent is the cozy dining niche, the dominant feature of which is an acquamarine glass sculpture wall; on left is an (unseen) glass display case. The stainless steel and glass coffee set is from anyroom.

Opposite
As in traditional Thai houses, the bed in Khun Wisit's bedroom is placed on the floor. On the right of the door is a large, concealed walk-in closet (unseen), while above a circular recess with fan provides visual appeal.

Above left
The apartment takes on different moods at different times of the day. "I like the light coming through the wooden blinds in the daytime," says the owner, "but during the evenings, the artificial light is good too." The niche at center houses a bentwood branch and light sculpture (partially unseen), designed by the architect himself.

Above right
As with other parts of the apartment, the bathroom is space-saving and well designed. Traditional Thai vessels are displayed on glass shelves and a rustic wood bowl sits atop the vanity counter.

NATURAL ORGANICS

Below
On the *lanai* (or verandah) a round glass side table with chunky cluster bamboo legs designed by Budji Layug is flanked by two woven *abaca* rope upright chairs with *tanguile* wood legs. On the table is a marble egg sculpture by Impy Pilapil. In the background a stand of delicate bamboo sprouts from a bed of river pebbles.

Right
The living room is set up as one would organize an informal relaxing room at home. A polished bamboo laminate coffee table designed by Budji Layug is surrounded by Kenneth Cobonpue's Tilt sofa and armchair with *abaca* cushions. On the table are a green-and-gold lacquer candleholder and two pewter candlesticks. The abstract painting is by leading artist Norberto "Lito" Carating, while the unusual z-shaped side table is also made from bamboo laminate.

Thankfully the days of uniform shops and warehouses with goods stacked up on shelves in regimented lines seem to be over. Save for the supermarket, stores — be they for fashion, interiors, gifts or others — are becoming increasingly imaginative. Take the Bangkok showroom of Filipino furniture designers Budji Living, for example: all the items for sale are situated in a 1960s house in Thonglor, Sukhumvit, with various rooms, patio, bar, and garden with pond intact. Meander round the house with its open layout, and you'll get a far better idea of how pieces look in situ than you ever would in a traditional shop.

It's surprising that more people aren't doing it really. It is sound sales-wise, and because the house has an airy, homey feel, clients are immediately comfortable with the surroundings. The wonderful furniture on show simply complements this comfort level. You're invited to wander at will — lie down on a bed, check out a chair, even relax with a cool drink for a while on the breezy *lanai* (terrace).

Budji Living is the brainchild of Antonio "Budji" Layug, a multi-talented designer who was responsible for putting together a group of eight Filipino designers in the late 1990s. Called Movement 8, their work was brought to world attention at a furnishing exhibition in Spain in 1999. In large part utilizing native materials — hardwood and hemp, bamboo, rattan, *abaca* and more — the designs combine expert craftsmanship with sleek lines and modern styles. Primarily aimed at the global market, Budji Living stocks pieces from many of these top designers, artists and artisans.

"A total design approach from exterior to interior is essential in creating a style that will endure the passage of time," says Layug. This is especially true in the tropics, and every "room" at Budji Living speaks about the relationship between indoor and outdoor spaces. Casual placement of pieces, quality materials, plenty of air and light, wicker and wire vases with greenery and a white painted backdrop result in a fresh interpretation of the classic tropical home.

The showroom speaks volumes about easy living: it's clean, modern, uncluttered, logical. And it certainly beats a visit to the local mall.

Below
Matilda sofa and armchair in rattan-covered metal with loose muslin covered upholstery is a design well suited to the tropics. On the dark crocodile leather coffee table, the creamy translucence of abalone laminated chisel cut Verona marble vases complements dark eurycles leaves. An all-purpose four-compartment box made of tobacco leaf and stained red is also on the table. On the wall is a recycled paper collage artwork and on the leather side table a bowl-shaped brown paper artwork — both by Tes Pasola. The standing floor lamp has a wenge wood base and white cloth shade. In the background, a huge chest of polished bamboo laminate has a deep red lacquer fruit bowl on top.

The open-sided verandah (or *lanai* as it is known in the Philippines) acts as the perfect show space for top-quality and durable garden furniture. Here a tropical-modern Cocoon loveseat and coffee table in metal wire weave by jewelry designer turned furniture maker Ann Pamintuan sit behind a black lacquer ottoman. Huge planters and a leafy garden complete the tropical scene.

Above
A Suzy Wong bed with screen made of *buri*, rattan and metal wire underneath is cozy chic. In the foreground is an Ernest wicker ottoman.

Right
One of the latest lines from Budji Layug is the Bettina rattan lounge chair and ottoman — here seen in an attractive green. On either side is an *abaca* laminate side table with tobacco leaf vase on top and (partially unseen) a huge black lacquer bowl. In the background the screen is one of Silk Cocoon's *abaca*-and-silk fabrics woven with thin bamboo poles.

Far right
Tilt armchair with natural cotton upholstery.

Budji Layug has a deep commitment to organic forms and materials especially those found in his native Philippines, and stocks many designs from Filipino artists that display a fresh interpretation of these forms to produce uniquely modern designs.

Clockwise from top left
Close-up of a large round wire vase designed by Movement 8's Ann Pamintuan; called the Lasso line, the vases come in barrel and round shapes and have the fragile texture of ribbons of seaweed. *Abaca* cushions delicately designed with miniature coco beads by Maricris Brias of Tadeco; *abaca* is a banana fiber known as Manila hemp. Close-up of the fine workmanship on a Coccon loveseat and Miro II boxy side table in textured crushed bamboo laminate. The spiral pattern on Ann Pamintuan's oversized Cocoon lounge chair; made of welded iron, it won the grand prix in metal design in Stockholm in 2003. Close-up view of a corner of the Tilt armchair designed by Kenneth Cobonpue in walnut. Close-up of the detailed weave on the Suzy Wong bed screen.

COLLECTION BOX

Full of filtered light, the living room is homely and home to some highly individual pieces of furniture. Modular sofa seating on the perimeter nestles round a meditation platform seat in elm wood, Shanshi, early 18th century, bought in Hong Kong. On right is a Shanghai-style standing lamp with yellow shade, also late 18th century. The dog in the foreground is a teakwood *soi* dog, bought at Lotus Gallery. "It's the nearest I ever came to owning a pet!" quips the owner. The checked carpet is from Tibet.

When Masa and Michael Unsworth acquired this duplex penthouse in a high-rise apartment block in the heart of Bangkok's business center, it was literally just a shell. They wanted a base in Bangkok — one that was high, central and could be molded to their own taste — and this fit the bill. "It was the only unfinished apartment in the building," explains Masa, "so my husband and I could start from scratch — choose our own layout, materials and so on."

Enlisting the help of interior designer Attayut Piranivich, Masa created a large living-dining room downstairs, and two bedrooms and a study upstairs. It's a warm, cosy series of spaces that works both as a very personal home and a showcase for her collection of Chinese and Japanese furniture and modern Chinese paintings. The feeling is airy and light, although as the apartment is north facing it is never in direct sunshine. It also seems larger than it actually is, as mirrors create the illusion of depth and more space.

Downstairs, the combination of white marble floors and cream-colored walls acts as the perfect canvas to showcase Masa's art. This ranges from some serious collector's pieces to items like kitschy Chinese pottery figurines celebrating the Cultural Revolution — now displayed in the bathroom. Niches with subtle, concealed lighting in walls and at floor level work as great display cases for sculptural pieces, while white Venetian blinds create just the right backdrop for colorful modern paintings. Clean-lined pieces of furniture such as the Italian oak dining table and straight-backed chairs and the low coffee table (a large meditation platform dating from the 18th century) are sleek and elegant. Upstairs, furniture was custom designed by Attayut Piranivitch's carpenters to keep rooms clutter free.

An added attraction is the apartment's breezy balcony that affords wonderful views over the city. Teak decking, a leafy pergola and plenty of plants make this a great spot for a breath of fresh air. Masa, who also owns homes in London and Croatia, likes to offer guests drinks here before dinner. "Life on the 31st floor gives a feeling of calm and isolation," she says, "but there is also a buzz as we are right in the middle of this enormous city."

Left
The partially obscured painting in the dining room of a blue bowl on gold leaf was bought in Hong Kong in 1998, artist unknown. On the dark wood dining table is an arrangement formed from circular coconut leaves and yellow spider chrysanthemums in a series of black ceramic square trays.

Right
The leafy deck features plumeria and bougainvillea as well as other ornamentals in planter boxes, and affords superb views over the city.

Right
The custom-made niche shelving is a specialty of interior designer Attayut Piranivich — it makes for a sweet display case and is also space saving.

Far right
A duo of lute and flute players, Han dynasty (206 BC– 220 AD), bought in Hong Kong.

Below
Custom-built dark wood furniture in the spare bedroom is streamlined chic. Atop the cabinet are two Burmese lacquerware containers and two small paintings by Vietnamese artist Cuong.

Masa believes that collecting doesn't always have to be serious, and she loves to browse in markets around the world.

Clockwise from top left
Three Chinese wise men incense holders, bought in the Beijing Thieves market one freezing Sunday morning. They sit on a Japanese red lacquer paulonia wood chest of drawers. Lime green lacquer plate with a coral and silver necklace from Tibet. The head in the background is in terracotta; it is of Masa, aged five, and was executed by her mother, a ceramic artist. A lovely example of a Mandarin collar box, used to store the collar of a Mandarin official. "Tattoo," an oil on canvas, (1994), by Jue Min Jun, a Beijing artist. Jue has had many solo and group exhibitions in southeast Asia, Europe and the USA and his paintings always feature a laughing man, or a group of laughing men — whether it is a big laugh, a crazy laugh, a near-death laugh or a laugh about society in general.

A FRESH OUTLOOK

Right
A mix of wood and clever lighting keeps the house looking spacious and clean. The veneer standing lamp is by Jiraphan Kitisasikultorn from Able Interior Workshop. Khun Jiraphan is an interior designer turned product designer who exports homewares and furniture under the label Touchable. This lamp, and the one on the work surface in the kitchen, are part of her 2004 collection. Opposite is a limestone wall with patterning and a rough wood wall: the textures of both are brought out by the lamp's rays.

Below
Making a splashy entrance by the front door is a Sputnik armchair made from fiberglass with a gold leaf mosaic finish by Eggarat Wongcharit from Craft Factor. It goes well with the yellow-toned painting above by Chinese artist Zhang Donghong.

Keeping things uncomplicated, clean and uncluttered, yet practical and comfortable too, is the aim of many a family home. For this couple with two small children, it seemed a simple enough desire. The residence was the former home of the husband's and the interior designer of choice, a company called Gimmick Design. Their brief was to create a child-friendly open airy interior, all the while retaining the homely feeling from the past but updating the facilities to meet the needs of the new inhabitants.

Sounds easy? It wasn't. For a start, everything had to be child-proofed. The clients, Kritsada and Amparin Tanvilai, wanted to be able to play with the children all over the house. Secondly, Khun Amparin wanted a "snug and cosy home that wasn't too modern," but also wanted light, garden views, an open-plan concept and a variety of textures. Gimmick had to work very closely with their clients to achieve the look and feeling they wanted.

Preferring to call themselves "interior creators" as they advise on all aspects of a project from architecture to interior design, lighting and furniture, staff at Gimmick pride themselves on achieving their clients' dreams. The design team opened out the ground floor into a semi open-plan space and put in floor-to-ceiling windows (with no curtains) to invite in garden views. The basement was left as is, and upstairs are the bedrooms, bathrooms and a library.

Flooring of limestone and teak wood is hard wearing, while walls are clean — perfect for a couple of choice artworks. The atmosphere is bright and lively and there are some unusual features, such as frosted glass lighting on stair rungs, inset handrail, natural stone walls with geometric patterning and wooden ceiling detail in the dining area. Eschewing aluminum in the kitchen for wood, and using terrazzo, glass and oak in the cloakroom was inspired, contributing in no small part to the homey ambience.

"When I came home feeling tired," says Khun Amparin, "I go through the front door and feel my energy coming back. The fresh colors, light from the large window and kids in the garden lift my spirit." Maybe the old adage — an open heart, a lot of love and a warm feeling are all you need in a family home — is true after all.

Right
Employing "fresh ideas and an intrinsic aesthetic" is the aim of Gimmick Design: the underlit stairs and inset handrail are innovative, as well as practical.

Far right
A tightly packed bunch of hand-tied carnations in deep red, chosen by Khun Sakul to bring out the red in the painting on the far wall (see right) sit on the dining room table in a glass vase.

Left

The living room, with French doors and windows giving direct access to the garden, is not too crowded. A modern dark-upholstered sofa is flanked by a fiberglass chair with an inflatable rubber base by Eggarat Wongcharit (on left) and a rocking chair with a wooden mosaic finish by the same designer (on right). The extraordinary chair is called the Bouncing Betty. In front is a round handmade rug in natural fibers by Rapee Leelasiri from Graph-TEX Studio. Huge *Monstera deliciosa* leaves in wooden vases are kept fresh with the addition of a concealed glass jar filled with water inside.

Right

Neutral tones and natural wood characterize the compact dining area. The table and boxy chairs are in white oak and come from B&B Italia. In the foreground, the woven rattan fruit bowl with wooden middle is by Udom Udomsrianan for Planet 2001.

Oppisite
"Renovating the house turned out to be very difficult, as we wanted to keep an old feeling from the past, but also make the house practical for our growing kids," says Khun Amparin. Nonetheless, the design proved successful, with homely touches in such places as this downstairs bathroom. The use of wood shelving and slatted wooden towel rails as well as terrazzo has resulted in a restful, yet easy to maintain, space.

This page, clockwise from top left
Herbal bath products from Juku, a Bangkok company that specializes in organic, natural gift products. Scented organic ball from Juku used to perfume the bathroom. Two "1001 Night" gold leaf mosaic vases by Eggarat Wongcharit. Tabletop lamp by Jiraphan Kitisasikultorn from Able Interior Workshop in the kitchen. Herbal soaps from Juku. Scented pot pourri in the bathroom.

DRAMA

Taking their cue from custom and culture, these up-to-the-minute spaces are imbued with drama. Rich hues, bold colors and sumptuous textiles combine with Oriental antiques and custom-crafted modern pieces to produce highly individual interiors. Be it a bar, shop, home or house, Asian heritage is celebrated, lauded and applauded — yet imaginatively reworked in a contemporary idiom.

HIGH DRAMA

Below
Overlooking the living space is a semi-open mezzanine lounging area with very low green-and-white seating and a bold painting by Symon, an expatriate artist in Bali whose work is popular in Bangkok. Hand woven mat and cushions by Ploenchan Vinyaratn Pornsurat of Beyond Living were carefully chosen to complement the bold colors of the painting.

British-based interior designer Kelly Hoppen was probably the first person to truly internationalize an East meets West aesthetic in the contemporary home. Combining Asian art, artefacts, furniture, fabrics and styles with Western know-how, craftsmanship and classic designs, she produces spaces that are clean-lined and simple, yet exotic and even opulent. And even though she didn't have anything to do with the penthouse of Somchai Piraban and Brian Renaud, many of her ideas and concepts are showcased in their home.

Overall, the apartment sports a pan-Asian aesthetic that is tactile and sensuous. Decorated and designed by the owners with the help of a designer, the spaces reflect a love of Oriental art. "Each room is a different variation of one central theme," explains Khun Somchai, "and that theme is an overall contemporary Asian feel. We achieve it by mixing Asian art and antiques with modern design elements."

This is evident as soon as you enter: in the small foyer the tone is set by a gold leaf panel and modernist Ikebana flower arrangement — controlled luxe you could say. This is continued into the spacious, high-ceilinged living room where an impressive view of the city skyline vies for attention with teak floors and modern Italian furniture. Off this room is an exceptionally elegant, formal dining room where wood-paneled walls taken from a traditional wooden Thai house surround a sleek table above which hangs an Italian chandelier with pale yellow shades. This casts inviting light over the table which is further illuminated by a back-lit display of antique Southeast Asian, Chinese, Korean and Japanese ceramics and modern glass pieces from Venice, Vancouver, Sydney and New York. "The collection is a work in progress," explain the owners, "and keeps up the theme of blending contemporary Western items with antique Asian ones." Hoppen would approve!

The penthouse's private quarters are no less thoughtfully executed: A masculine, clubby study sports black leather furniture, dark woven reed matting on the walls, and an enormous collection of books. Bedrooms are stylish and smart (the guest one having a Japanese aesthetic, the master bedroom a combo of dark wood and hot pink), while the bathrooms have to be seen to be believed.

Left
Boxy black leather armchairs in the masculine study are Italian, but appealed to the owners because they resemble chairs from a formal Chinese room. An antique rug, stingray-skin and gold-and-red silk poufs from Lotus Arts de Vivre and pink cushions from Jim Thompson, work well with floor-to-ceiling bookcases. Here you'll find a complete cloth-bound collection of the Everyman Library, 300 books issued as a collection of the greatest works of Western literature, as well as books on art, architecture and travel.

Below
Bold colors and a mix of modern and antique pieces characterize the airy living room. In the foreground are two 150-year-old lacquered elm wood Ming chairs with bright cerise silk cushions from Jim Thompson. The walls sport panels inset with woven reed matting in black.

Left
The dining table is crafted from one large solid slab of teak wood and sports a sunny daffodil and candle arrangement complementing the chandelier. Daffodils and candles are secured in black ceramic square trays with a *kenzan*, a lead and nail spike device inspired by Japanese Ikebana.

Below
A dark wooden console and gold leaf panel gives an Oriental Zen-like welcome to the stylish abode. Atop the console is a Japanese-inspired stainless steel tray by Sakul Intakul, adorned with golden protea in an Ikebana-style arrangement.

Left
In the Thai-style master bedroom light green silk covers one wall and the ceiling has teak beams, but pride of place goes to the contemporary four-poster bed with rich silk duvet cover and cushions by Jim Thompson. Silk lampshades on either side of the bed are designed by Ou Baholyodhin for Jim Thompson. A custom-made metal framed mirror makes a strong statement in this dramatic room.

Below
An overhead spotlight above a daybed casts illumination on to gorgeous gold, pink and orange silk cushions from Jim Thompson. Set against an orange painted wall, this corner niche is on one side of the bedroom.

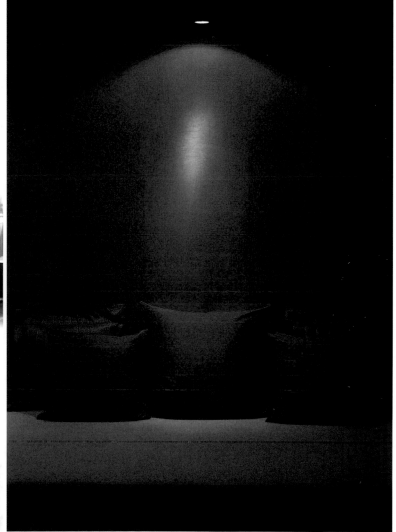

Right

In the master bathroom, exposed brick walls and a cool stone floor are juxtaposed with modern basins and inset mirrors — a classic East meets West combo.

Below

The downstairs powder room sports a commissioned rural mural painted by a professor and his students from Thailand's premier fine arts school, Silapakorn University. Kitsch — yet totally cool — it features a rice field and *klong*; accompanied by an earthen jar used as a washbasin and old teak wood planks covering the floor, it makes for an unusual bathroom in an urban setting. A nude on right (unseen) — of a boy about to take a bath with a towel in his hand — is also by Symon.

Right
Sliding windows with rice paper panels give the guest bedroom a Zen air. An antique *obi* (Japanese sash), Chinese silk cushions, slender lantern-style bedside lamps and lamp with rice paper shade complete the Japanese theme.

Far left
Custom-designed by a carpenter in Bangkok, the geometric windows take their inspiration from Japanese *shoji* or sliding doors, the panels of which were covered in translucent rice paper. These served the dual purpose of allowing natural, filtered light to enter a room, while also protecting owners' privacy.

Left
A close-up of the intricate workmanship on the *obi*.

Japanese influences are apparent in many areas of this apartment: White river pebbles and grey slate in the guest bathroom. Swirling free-form metal tray from Beyond Living on a stingray skin and gold leaf Seiki Torige tabletop. Stacked aquamarine glass sheets are the basis for the elegant, curved legs of the Torige table. A modern calla lily arrangement in a white square receptacle with Ikebana spikes by Sakul Intakul is in keeping with the Japanese themed spare bedroom.

SKY HIGH

Below
The design of both bar and restaurant was oriented towards nighttime effects, says Scott Whittaker of DWP Cityspace. Illuminated steps, underlit cupola lights, tall stacked glass column lighting and of course the under bar counter all cast light on the fairytale setting.

When the hot, dusty wind known as the sirocco sweeps up across the Mediterranean from north Africa, it's said that people are unable to sleep. The weather changes, and a kind of restlessness and drama enter the atmosphere. Apt then, that this open-air restaurant atop a monumental skyscraper in Bangkok takes its name from this meteorological phenomenon. For Sirocco serves Mediterranean fare, it is often breezy and blowy, and it stays open until late.

Part of the neo-classical Dome complex atop the megalithic downtown State Tower building, Sirocco and its dramatically lit Sky Bar are only open during the evenings. It is the perfect venue for a sundowner or two. With an almost 360 degree panorama overlooking the entire city, views are breathtaking. Access is via an enormous, under-lit dome on the 65th floor: from here you can make a splashy entrance down a sweeping Spanish Steps-type staircase to the al fresco dining space below. Tables are dressed in white cottons and lit by elegant fiberglass cupolas on pedestals — and the sound of champagne corks popping is not uncommon.

Views back up to the opulent rotunda are almost as extraordinary as the cyclorama unfolding around. The luminous bar, set to one side on what appears to be a promontory, is furnished with a state-of-the-art lighting system whereby its base changes from neon pink to green to turquoise, matching the fluorescent cocktails set on its marble counter-top. As one patron, an executive from Hong Kong, exclaimed: "The whole place emits a feeling of Hollywood: it feels like we're on a movie set!"

Interior design company DWP Cityspace was entrusted with the design of the complex — and sensibly allowed Sirocco's setting and situation to take center stage. As the Dome was already part of the architecture, they decided to retain the Italianate style in some of the other features. "Both Sirocco and the other venues around the Dome were designed around ideas of Italy, for example the steps and fountain were reminiscent of Rome; it's not a literal interpretation but a film set version of Rome, as in the movie 'La Dolce Vita'." He adds that his team had a lot of fun creating such an extravagant venue — and are pleased with the over-the-top result.

Left
Nightime views are certainly a big attraction at Sirocco, but many customers come for the live jazz musicians on a podium above and wonderful Italian fare from chef Stefano, previously at Phuket's Amanpuri.

Below
The spherical Sky Bar sits on a broad wooden deck. The viewing platform behind is not for the faint hearted.

Left

The Italianate Dome as seen from the bar. Although vertigo inducing, the steps are well lit. The cupola bowls (seen on the previous page) were designed "to give scale and a bit of fantasy as well as a way to provide diffused lighting," says designer Scott Whittaker.

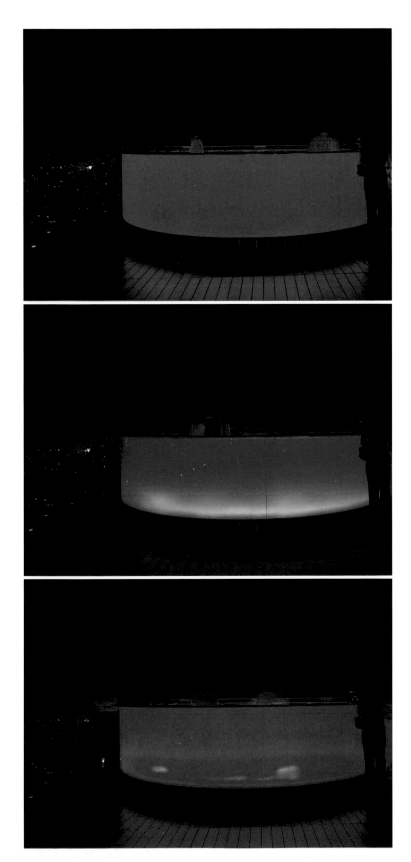

Left and above

Neon alternatives at the Sky Bar. In addition to this bar and restaurant, the Dome Complex offers a corporate room in a perfect circle located on the 67th floor in the rotunda itself, a cigar bar called Distil and another restaurant by the name of Mezzaluna. After all, it is the second tallest building in Thailand.

HEAVEN SENT

The global trend for the boutique bistro can probably be traced back to the early 1990s when London's chic superstore Harvey Nicks opened Fifth Floor, their creative eatery with a celeb clientele. After that, everyone jumped on the bandwagon. DKNY wouldn't be the same nowadays without its cappuccino-and-cake café, and Ralph Lauren is as well known for its lifestyle section as it is for apparel. Even lower-market brand stores such as Australia's Country Road, America's Borders' bookstores and Singapore's Blood Bros have bistros, lifestyle sections and bars to boot.

So, when four interior and graphic designers opened a four-in-one concept store in Bangkok's Gaysorn Plaza, it was a logical extension of the trend. Here a bar shares space with a bookshop, a home décor shop and a fashion atelier. Each is stocked with an eclectic range of high quality products, hand-picked or designed by the owners for both their quality and their quirkiness, in an environment that is suitably exotic.

The store is certainly theatrical. Computer-controlled lighting ensures that a mysterious, yet welcoming, atmosphere permeates throughout: back-lit display alcoves, reminiscent of *tokonoma* in Zen temples, change lighting color according to the time of the day while spots from above illuminate certain sections. "Viyahas means atmosphere, sky, heaven and open space," explains one of the owners Prakit Woraprasit, "So we used the symbol of atmosphere to represent our shop, like an eye."

The warm lighting combined with unusual textures — raw cement walls, polished cement floors, warm wood parquet flooring — and custom-made display cabinets showcase the well-chosen wares in an imaginative and innovative manner. Even though there is 280 square meters (3,000 square feet) of space, the overall feel is of an intimate lounge. Browsing (and buying) can be followed by a snack in the Bhargas Bar, where faux fur seating, glass-and-chrome tables and candlelight create a suitably Bohemian ambience.

After all, it's no secret that retail is therapy; and therapy should always be accompanied by nurturing eating and drinking. If you can do all under the same roof — so much the better.

Left
"Look good — taste good — feel good" is the strapline at Vihayas, and true to their word, the owners at this Eastern Emporium offer beauty, sustenance, flair and fashion all under one roof. At the entrance a roughly rendered unfinished cement wall sports the shop sign in relief. Both the square and round poufs at center are made from leather with rattan detailing.

The back wall in the bar was designed with purple and green arcylic pieces, inspired by the reflection one sees from a church window. Bar chairs by Paninya Hiranyaked.

This page, clockwise from top left
Items designed and made by the Vihayas Design Group are chosen with care and displayed in an imaginative manner. A cute, yet practical, breakfast tray made from wood with receptacles for coffee, cookies, bread, jam and so on. There is even a slot to hold a newspaper. Ceramic vases and plates, the recipient of a design award from Elle Decoration magazine in 2003. Ceramic sculpture, a bold shape for a display case. Mother-of-pearl lamp and tray is sleek and slimline.

HIGH-STYLE GLAMOUR

Originally envisaged as a compact pied-à-terre in town for a couple whose main home was in northern Thailand, this apartment occupies a prime position in the city center. Measuring 124 square meters (1,335 sq ft), it comprises two one-bedroom units that have been knocked together. Hence, the apartment is long and slim, with all rooms having views over adjacent Lumpini Park and the city skyline.

The fact that the owners have now sold their country home and moved full-time to the city has not changed a thing. They wanted to downsize — physically and mentally — after years of living surrounded by antiques, objects d'art and clutter and dogged by maintenance and staffing issues. Hence, the apartment is clean lined and semi modern with only a few choice artifacts — and very easy to run. "We always feel relaxed and cozy in our little nest," explains Wongvipa Devahastin na Ayudhya, "and because we have this great view over the green park, we don't feel hemmed in."

Incorporating a large living/dining room and sleek open kitchen, with two bedrooms at opposite ends of the apartment, the layout is linear. On entering, the first thing you see is a stunning aqua-blue sculpture by glass artist Seiki Torige; on one side of it is the living area and one bedroom, at the other is the dining room and open kitchen and the second bedroom. The overall impression is of understated drama — lush teak wood floors, light streaming through slatted shutters, luxe fabrics and stunning artwork.

"Even though the apartment is fairly modern," explains the owner, "we've created quite a homey feeling with natural materials such as split bamboo and teak wood, both of which were common in old Thai houses. Furthermore, we've incorporated organics into the interior: cushion covers in hemp, fine woven rattan dining chairs, linen bedspreads, floral arrangements, aromatic candles and oil burners — all these contribute to a natural feeling inside."

Natural maybe, but we're talking high-style natural here. Choice artifacts, exquisite tableware, clever lighting and an eye for every detail have resulted in a warm home, as well as a design-conscious and successful interior. Meticulous planning and an inherent sense of style have worked well in the small space.

Left
The light honey-colored Italian marble table from Casa Bella works well with fine woven rattan with teak frame chairs from Pataya Furniture Collection. The abstract artwork behind by Thawatchai Somkong is entitled "Back to Original."

Below
Separating the dining and living areas is a large glass sculpture by Seike Torige called "Ladies" on a soap-stone pedestal. Tea lights behind make for a flickering candle effect.

Opposite
Antique Chinese wedding cabinet from Tomlinson Gallery is situated on left as guests enter the apartment. Aside it is a woven rattan stool that doubles up as a lamp by Udom Udomsrianan from Planet 2001; it was purchased at Panta, his outlet at Siam Discovery. A couple of stems of gloriosa lilies sit atop the cabinet in two glass vases designed by Christian Tortu. The Tibetan tiger rug is from Lotus Arts de Vivre.

Right
Japanese lacquerware containers with single peonies have a Zen minimalist effect on the clean laid dining table. Lacquer bowls, plates with red peony motif and spoons are all from Japan, while the custom-made lacquer chopsticks are from Living Space. White Celadon square dinner plates with gold motif are custom made by Ceram Thai.

Far left
Mouth-blown glasses with white spiral pattern from Union Victors sit before a celadon sake jug.

Left
White celadon square dinner plates with gold motif are custom made by Ceram Thai.

Right
An antique Chinese gilded wood carved mirror with bamboo pattern from Hong Kong sits above a custom-made teak dressing table from Chiang Mai and rattan and teak chair from Pataya Furniture Collection.

Far right
A mass of gloriosa lilies in an acrylic tank from Cocoon were chosen for this corner, as their color matches the adjacent painting (unseen, opposite) beautifully.

Below
The master bedroom has leather cushions and a patch-work bedcover by Gilles Caffier from Orok's Co Ltd. An antique Chinese lacquer screen from Shianghai above the bed was purchased in Hong Kong — and gives the room further exotic cachet.

Above
Single peony and lacquer bowl arrangement as before.

Right
The intimate lounge features a boxy teak sofa with hemp and linen cushions from Cocoon. Behind are custom-designed sliding doors made from split bamboo with a teak frame, inspired by traditional opium matting. The wooden shutters keep out the heat of the day.

In small spaces, it is the details the really count. Full credit must go to the owner for choosiing quality items that give the intimate space such style and panache.

Clockwise from top left
The owner often eschews electricity for candles and tea lights in glass containers. Two poufs, one in black plaited leather and the other in red lizard stamped leather, from Leather Paragon. Single stem gloriosa lily in UNESCO-award winning Sakul Intakul "tri-pod" bronze vessel. Traditional Japanese tray with stack of lacquered cups and elegant pot used for serving and drinking sake.

CANDY COLOR

Below
The shape of low-level lime green chairs is echoed in the circular coffee table in a breakout area from the Jungle-themed 21st floor.

Right
Deep blue acrylic containers from Habitat on a stainless steel bar counter in the Plum section contain pink gerberas cocooned in a leaf wrap; they complement the mauve bar front and large grape installation behind.

Banning the office blues and replacing them with bright, multi-colored, flexible spaces was the design brief. Eight floors in a downtown office building was the location. Hutchison Wireless was the client. DWP Cityspace was the creative team behind the transformation. And the result?

A bold departure from the usual grey office environment. Ignoring all preconceptions about working spaces, the designers took the back office pantry/staff room and made it the primary focus on each floor. From this interactive hub radiate different permutations of open and closed meeting rooms, breakout areas using wireless technology, and seating clusters. The whole ethos is one of communication — a notable (and sensible) milieu for a telecoms company.

The overall effect is more café culture than corporate culture. Each of the eight floors has a different color code: this reflects the company's corporate identity based around a triangular symbol with changing colors. The colors were chosen to stimulate staff and clients as well as provide visual identity to each group. In addition to the primary colors, there are bold graphics of different fruits in strategic places. It's a far cry from the cubby-hole offices of the past.

Each of Hutchison's office floors has a different, highly individual character. The pantone panorama covers red, purple, orange, yellow, green and blue — so there are Cherry, Plum, Tangerine, Cheese, Jungle or Lagoon workers. Only the general reception and executive offices have been left sober and serious. The dynamic environment is further enhanced by modern signage, clean-lined Italian furniture, quirky slogans on the walls, and excellent and funky lighting.

In the past decade or so, some firms have begun to cotton on to the fact that people don't like working in dull, beige or grey cubicles. In the highly competitive telecoms industry, Hutchison management felt that the new offices would help retain workers and increase productivity in a business where staff turnover is quite high. Hence the emphasis on comfort and relaxation — it's a trend to be encouraged.

Opposite
Colorful graphics and even prominent signage on meeting room doors and walls is complemented by the shape of modernist chairs.

Right
An industrial-style circular ceiling sculpture of painted MDF hangers with exposed air ducts behind hangs above and echoes the shape of a dividing wall. Hanging lamps in metal and plastic sheeting, steel-legged chairs and a cool granite floor contribute to the rugged feeling.

Far right
A peeling from the trunk of the spider lily forms the sheath within an acrylic container from Habitat for a single white chrysanthemum. Placed side by side with an identical partner, it makes a striking, clean arrangement.

Welcome.

Left
A semi circular reception counter is sited below a similar shaped circular light fitting above.

Large plasma screens and Italian designed chairs and tables along with state-of-the-art lighting and clean light timber floors ensure offices are airy, comfortable and spacious.

Left
The executive rooms and reception are the only floors where the color scheme is more conventional. Here, in the Jungle section, brown and green are used to striking effect.

Right
Giant graphics of kiwi fruits characterize the Jungle floor. Here orange gerberas, evenly cut young coconut leaves and bright orange acrylic vases from Habitat contrast with the color scheme. The varying in height and haphazard placement of vases is asymmetric and intentional.

Giant green apple on a stain-less steel bar counter gives a fresh, healthy feel.

Left
The Cheese floor painted in pale lemon and off white appropriately sports yellow chrysanthemums in tall acrylic vases from Habitat on a bar counter. Coconut leaves form the protective support. Tall black vinyl and steel bar stools are used throughout.

WHITE OUT

When Russian artist Kasimir Malevich (1878–1935) showcased his White on White series of paintings in 1918 to an astounded Moscow public, he couldn't have had any idea of how influential his work would become. Comprising mainly white oils on white canvases, the paintings reflected his purist ideals of absolute austerity — and went on to influence abstract artists both in Russia and abroad.

Over the following decades we've seen numerous offshoots of his original — white-clad skyscrapers, minimalist interiors, the white rubber cat suit, white leather and blond hair, the white plastic domed iMac and iPod, the white box CD player… and most recently the Bed Supperclub in Bangkok. Here white-on-white has been elevated into a venue for all the arts — culinary, visual, musical and theatrical.

Housed in a futuristic 800 sq-m (8,610 sq-ft) tubular construction, more spaceship than building, the Bed Supperclub is an architectural one-off. The brainchild of a group of creatives, the idea was to build premises that embodied "freedom, beauty, the exotic and the bizarre" along with a healthy dose of fun. Securing the services of Orbit Design Studio, the group transferred their ideas into reality. The tube is divided in two parts: a fine-food dining and reclining section and a more fluid club section, where black-and-white movies are projected on the ceiling and top djs spin their discs.

The restaurant is the focus of these photos: here crisp white sheets on freshly-made beds, plumped-up pillows and cushions provide diners with a cosy semi-horizontal space. Even crockery and modernist versions of the Thai *khantoke* or tray table are white, creating a blank canvas against which other senses are heightened.

Bed Supperclub has had Bangkok's chattering classes flocking to it in their droves. It has also caught the attention of international style mavens: UK magazine *Wallpaper** saw fit to feature it and *Condé Nast Traveler* (April 2003) voted the venue as one of 7 New Modern Architectural Wonders of the World. When it first opened in 2003, it was literally swamped. However, this is no short-term phenomenon. Food, music, décor and ambience have an extremely international feel here, and for sheer daring, the owners get full marks. For innovation, ditto. And for comfort? ZZZzzzzzz.

Left
The club's steel-clad exterior with its cylindrical tunnel form has its head in the clouds, but its structural supports firmly on the ground. Vaguely resembling a hovering UFO, its modular construction system allowed for easy assembly.

Below
Shades of pale: Softly padded white walls, comfy lounging cushions and modernist *khantoke* tray tables with Sakul Intakul small interconnecting "tamarind" porcelain vessels with a single white orchid in each are seductive chic.

Supine style: Upholstered white "beds" run the length of either side of the restaurant, while an industrial-style staircase and upper balcony contribute to the spaceship-style effect. On the ground floor iconic dining chairs made from one piece of acrylic resin and tables with softly-rounded corners give upright diners an edge.

Guests are encouraged to
lounge, loiter and linger —
all the while eating, drinking,
talking, looking and listening.
The central staircase allows
them to eat up or down.

Right
Surprisingly, once these
orchids are spray painted,
they can last for quite some
time before disintegrating.

Far left
Funky speakers suspended
from the ceiling and railings
play pre-programmed music
throughout the evening.

Left
Candles in square frosted
glass vessels are highly
stylized.

INTERNATIONAL APPEAL

It is wonderful what a good design company and a committed owner can achieve in what is architecturally a fairly ordinary 1970s town house in Bangkok. Built in two separate but adjacent structures, the smaller utilities section has a study, kitchen and dining room, while the larger building houses a large living room, three bedrooms and bathrooms. Before renovation, the house seemed cramped and hemmed in, despite the 1,200 square-meter (12,900 sq-ft) plot, half of which was garden. But once a few walls were removed, interior surfaces given a strong color palette, and the owner's belongings installed, the picture became quite different.

Design Plus, a Bangkok interior design firm, worked closely with the owner to achieve his vision of a lively but comfortable family home. There are a number of different textural finishes in the house — polished and painted concrete floors inset with tiles; painted Balinese doors; terracotta tiles lined with ceramic tiles; bamboo flooring; metal in parts of the ceiling; and exposed brick walls — always drawing the eye. Combined with this are an uninhibited color scheme and an unusual collection of tribal art and artifacts.

Even though the feeling is contemporary, this is no minimalist's dream home. Rather it reflects the personality of its owner in a refreshing and highly individual manner. There is an airy feeling of space: in order to open up views into the garden partition walls were removed and large swathes of glass installed. There is also a semi-industrial ethos with the use of exposed brick and pipe work. Center stage is given to the owner's eclectic collections: here a selection of African masks, there an Indonesian canoe transformed into a bookcase, and elsewhere original film posters that date from 1938 to 1966. For the bibliophile, the study is the Mecca: here 400 or more rare, old books about India, Churchill, World War 1 and golf are stacked from floor to ceiling.

Overall, it's a well thought through home, where comfort hasn't been compromised by design; rather, the spaces have been designed to be comfortable. "I enjoy living in an uncluttered series of living spaces," says the owner, "Even though I'm in the center of the city, it is very quiet and the landscape adds a strong earthy feel."

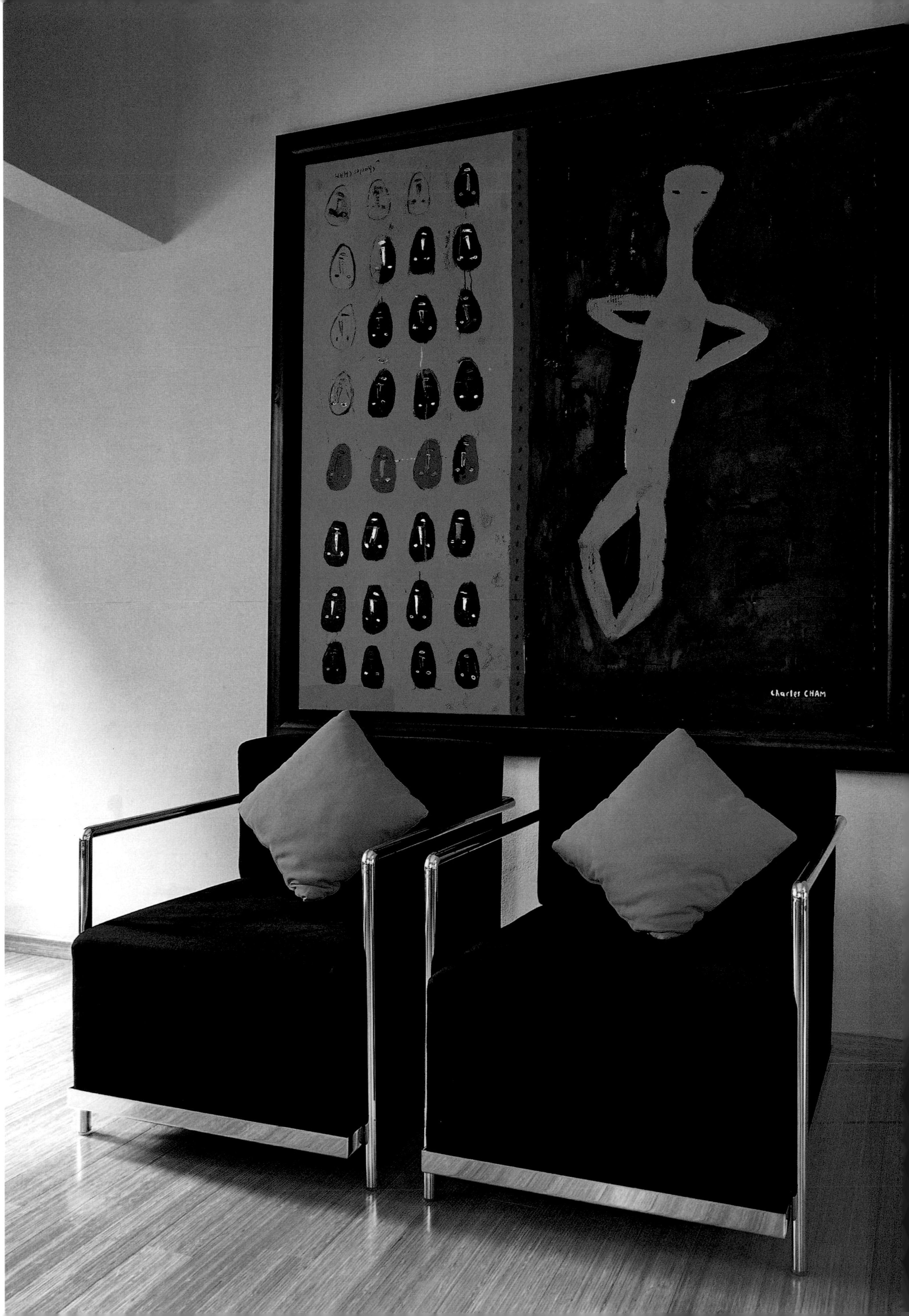
Charles CHAM

Garden views and plenty of light characterize the living room with its expansive built-in seating with *poleng* (black-and-white check) patterned cushions. The central low-level coffee table is Italian.

Left
Chosen to contrast with the color of Arthur's aqua-marine toned dining room, a hand-tied bunch of golden rod blooms is spherically arranged in a glass vase. Ceramic tiles and a turquoise painted border around the skylight are statement making. The large painting on the far wall is by Maitree Pharahom; called "Angel of the Ricefield," it was painted in 1994.

Below left
Close-up of the hand-fired turquoise-toned tiles set around the dining table in the terracotta tiled floor.

Below right
Grey river pebbles, inset with multi-colored tea lights, sit in an antique Balinese rice pounder.

Right
An exposed brick wall painted white contrasts with ocher walls and light wood floors to reveal a gallery-like space for some of the owner's art. The central painting of Chairman Mao is by Zhao Cong Sheng (2001) and is called "Mao series number 13." On left is a sculpture of a Dogon ladder from Burkina Faso in Africa; about 100 years old, it was bought at auction. On right is a wooden Bobo Mask from Central Africa. The rice pounder sits in front.

Above
The master bedroom is a riot of color: A Ghanaian Ashanti fabric that was used as a cape doubles up as a bedcover and a Navajo *serape* (cape) from the late 19th century hangs behind. On left is an acrylic (1992) by Krijono, a Javanese artist working in Bali.

Left
Strands of colorful beads hang on a hook on the back of the bathroom door.

Opposite
The master bathroom in black displays an eclectic collection of beadwork from Africa, Indonesia and Borneo. Mirrors enlarge the space.

Left
In spite of the city center location, the house has a large garden with mango trees and overhang of a huge rain tree from the next garden. A *balé* imported from Bali was reconstructed in Bangkok with a new roof made from copper; it has plenty of lounging space overlooking the lawn.

Below
Old Balinese doors brought to Bangkok and painted bright blue give access to the second-floor bedrooms.

Bottom
Moss-encrusted garden jar carved from lava stone is also from Bali.

Above
A small swimming pool is flanked by a border of river pebbles and a lush planting that includes crotons, palms and heliconias.

Right
The driveway is lined with exposed brick walls on both sides. An old bullock cart wheel from Chiang Mai gives a rustic feel and tall cactus grow on either side.

Space, texture, the outdoors, and a strong use of color are the strengths in this house, both inside and out.

Clockwise from top left
The swimming pool is edged with granite and pebbles. Golden rod blooms on a wooden slatted table. A planter with multiple strips spray painted bright green contrasts beautifully with the Balinese turquoise door. Close-up of the aquamarine swimming pool — cool, fresh and inviting.

SMALL IS BEAUTIFUL

Gimmick Design, a Bangkok studio that specializes in interior and
architectural design and space planning, was responsible for this
innovative, yet cosy, apartment. Commissioned by a young couple,
who only use the apartment on the weekends (they live during
the week in the larger family home), the brief was for a "cheerful,
convenient, relaxed and private pied-à-terre." Furthermore, the
couple wanted only one bedroom instead of the existing three, and
an open, roomy living area.

Gimmick rose to the challenge, and removed walls and rooms
to achieve the structural requirements. More importantly, they
incorporated a number of space-saving devices, and more than one
or two ambitious details. These succeeded in transforming what
could have been a rather ordinary small space into something eye-
catching, young and trendy.

The main feature that catches the eye wherever you are in the
apartment is the installation of six egg-shaped wooden panels that
separate the sleek white pantry from the living quarters. Described
as "moon doors" by the interior designers, they pivot 360 degrees,
so can be turned to any angle for access between the two rooms.
Even when totally closed, they allow glimpses through slats to the
next room — ensuring that a sense of continuity is retained. This
largesse is continued in the living/dining room.

Further enterprising features include sunken rectangular light
fixtures on the ceiling and wall of the foyer (very dramatic on entry);
four custom-designed and concealed shoe cabinets (traditionally
Thais remove their shoes on entering a home); a bright washroom
with yellow painted wooden panels and wood splash-backs; and
access to the bedroom through a tall, slim door that echoes the
shape of a Thai temple entry. These significant additions illustrate
how small details can transform an interior.

"My husband and I wanted the design to be different from our
family home," says owner Punjavadee Tanavilai, "We agreed we
wanted our apartment to be colorful and a little modern, but with a
touch of Asian spirit." It appears that Gimmick Design listened to
their clients.

Lighting is carefully chosen in this apartment: In the background on right, a sculptural hanging lamp whose circular motifs echo that of the shelves and round ceiling lights, is dramatic. The anglepoise standing lamp by Angus Hutcheson for Panta in the living section is no less statement making.

Above
Two temple-style doors on either side of a plasma screen, one of which leads from the cozy living space into the bedroom, are a take on old Thai style. Recessed ceiling lighting, polished wood floors, comfortable sofas in a restrained palette and large windows characterize the open-plan living section.

Right
Modular, slatted egg-shaped pivoting doors separate the living quarters from the kitchen. A change in floor color also helps to demarcate the space.

Opposite
The functional small kitchen has plenty of storage space.

Above and right
Diamond pattern silk chenille cushions and leather trimmed bedcover by Nagara for Jim Thompson give the bedroom textural appeal. The pattern is taken from traditional temple motifs and matches the temple-style bedroom door. A pair of stainless steel bedside lamps by Stephane W Sohneider for Panta are boxy chic. Venetian blinds shield sunlight while one wall is entirely coated in wood.

Far right
As the bedroom is quite small, the inbuilt wardrobe is space saving, as is the inclusion of a sofa bed.

Left
Slatted wood and clapboard give a refreshing feel in the powder room. The square sink and circular mirror complement the tiny mosaic tiled wet area perfectly.

Below left
Herbal soaps from Juku, a local Thai company that specializes in household and gift items.

Below right
A lime green cattleya bloom in a resin receptacle with stainless steel detailing from Sakul Intakul adds a feminine touch to the bathroom.

LIGHT AND SPACE

The modern mantra for tropical living is light and space. Space, both indoors and outdoors, is the ultimate commodity in the over-crowded East: when large floor plans are combined with high ceilings, open-air verandahs, floor-to-ceiling glass doors, open decks and plenty of natural light, they take on a life of their own. These interiors celebrate the cream of the crop in modern tropical living: bright, roomy, breezy and unabashedly individual, they're feng shui savvy too.

LOFTY SENTIMENTS

Below
An open-plan staircase connects the different levels in this house. As in the traditional shophouse configuration, the town-houses are long and thin, but with the incorporation of skylights and dominant shading devices as well as an internal atrium, seen here, they are not at all dark.

Opposite
Budji Layug made design waves in the early 1980s with a line of giant bamboo chairs, but then went on to utilize other indigenous Southeast Asian materials in innovative ways in his furniture designs. Harnessing the talent of seven other artists and artisans (who became known as Movement 8), he went on to open shops selling their work. In this room, two of Movement 8's designers are represented: Milo Naval has utilized a *sica* weave in an innovative modular sofa design, while Tes Pasola has used paper and bits of glass to produce the meditative artwork "Garlic."

This modern townhouse is part of a development of new housing in central Bangkok by architects DWP Cityspace. Called the Lofts Sathorn (as it is located off Sathorn Road), it comprises 25 homes in total. Built in clusters of four to five with a shared pool and garden area, each home nonetheless has its own car parking, entrance and private rear garden. Taking inspiration from Asian shophouses, the design is contemporary and clean.

This particular house has 420 square meters (4,520 sq ft) of space and is arranged over five floors, with each floor being part of a double height space. The utilities are housed on the lower floor, whilst the ground floor has a large living and dining room and an open-plan kitchen, as well as a mezzanine level (which can be closed off using sliding screens). There's a dramatic internal atrium at levels 4 and 5 that creates a wonderful feeling of space in the upper bedroom quarters. The stairs are lofty and open, as is the feeling in the entire house. A rooftop terrace is a bonus.

Aimed at Yuppie families, the homes in the Lofts Sathorn are designed to be low on maintenance, yet high on comfort. Materials were chosen carefully to be hassle-free. External screens providing shade are not timber as they appear, but are made from a concrete based board product called Conwood. The idea was to create a long-life screen that wouldn't be affected by the pollution in Bangkok. Flooring is in Vietnamese bamboo, while composite tiles in the bathrooms are easy to keep clean.

In keeping with the overall ethos of contemporary Asian living, most of the furniture in this house comes from the Bangkok outlet of Filipino designer Budji Layug. A strong modern look is achieved with oversized sofas, natural grass matting, meditative artworks and an emphasis on organics.

Most people in Bangkok live in a condominium or a detached house, so the Lofts Sathorn is a new concept for metropolitan living. Whittaker sums up: "This is an evolutionary design rather than a revolutionary one. It reflects the new lifestyle of people in Thailand that is urban and contemporary, but still tropical. As the pace of life increases in Bangkok, inner city living is increasingly desirable."

Left
The dining room is clean and spare with a glass-and-oak table by Kenneth Cobonpue and matching *hagkal*-weave *ikat* covered chairs. The table is given a splash of color by orange gerbera protruding from a nest of cut spider lily leaves in round glass containers and orange linen napkins. Above the console is a paper collage artwork by Tes Pasola, while two primitive wooden statues and a deep-red lacquer fruit bowl sit atop it.

Above
White glass cups with orange-colored interiors from Union Victors and gold-lacquer and inset woven mats from Asian Motif continue the warm theme in the dining room.

Above
The first-floor living room features a couple of Yin & Yang armchairs (on left) by Kenneth Cobonpue in split rattan and metal and a flat *abaca* weave daybed by Milo Naval (on right) on the other side of the coffee table. Spiralling reed mace offer drama in a sculptural arrangement in the corner; inset in cubist display cases is a collection of Thai ceramics.

Right
Close-up of chairs as above.

Far right
Close-up of Milo Naval's *sica* weave sofa.

Left
The façade of the house is designed to provide filtered light, as are the huge French windows that connect this balcony to a guest bedroom. Here a mock-wooden trellis, timber decking and potted plants, as well as a low coffee table and lounging sofa from Budji Living, give a relaxed, open-air feel.

Below
In the living room, a nest of dark *abaca* laminate coffee tables, lounging cushions and a low level console make for an attractive corner niche. Dark wood Venetian blinds filter harsh sunlight.

Above
This central courtyard leading off one of the bedrooms is visible from every level and takes its inspiration from the traditional shophouse lightwell. Tiled in slate, it is cool and quiet — and also serves the purpose of allowing light to enter the house.

Right
Kenneth Cobonpue's Croissant Easy Armchair made from *buri* (the core of the coconut leaf), steel and *abaca* is both comfortable and easy on the eye.

Far right
Milo Naval, known for his swirly, modernist Wave Bed, has designed a more conservative number here in *abaca* weave, with steel legs.

Right
Bathrooms are simple and easy to maintain with clean tiling, glass shower kiosks and modernist round sinks.

A PASSION FOR CHAIRS

Below
A corner niche features a futuristic lamp by Mario Botta atop a stand designed by Khun Tinakorn and red ilex in a yellow vase. Two Dafne folding chairs by Gastone Rinaldi for Thema (1980) are lined up against the wall on left.

As soon as you set eyes on the house of Khun Tinakorn Rujinarong, it is obvious that you are in an architect's house. Clean, spare, contemporary — and totally white, the house says as much about the spaces within the structure, as about the structure itself.

"I designed and did the interior of the house myself," explains Khun Tinakorn, "as a museum for my large collection of chairs, vases and coffee sets." The architect owns over 200 individual chairs, designed by luminaries such as Frank Lloyd Wright, Charles Eames and Joseph Hoffman amongst others. Many are on display in the large gallery-style space on the ground floor.

Built in an I-shape around a leafy courtyard, the family residence is made from concrete and painted white on both roof and walls. There are extra large ceramic tiles on the floors, and triangular, circular and square windows bring light into the angular two-story house. The strong architectural lines of a 25-meter (82-ft) stark façade are echoed within the house, highlighting a circular staircase at one end, a double-height ceiling and an upper walkway that runs the length of the house.

With three rooms downstairs and three upstairs, the house offers flexible spaces that can be interchanged at will. As most of Khun Tinakorn's artifacts and chairs date from the '50s and '60s, a retro feel predominates. This is accentuated by the primary colors of the objects themselves: bright red plastic chairs, rainbow-hued glasses and jugs, a sunshine yellow boxy table, an abstract canvas, a bright rug, and floral arrangements with sunflowers, yellow and pink gerbera and other sunny-hued blooms.

With the exception of the long dining table made from one piece of teakwood, furniture is funky, fun and slightly tongue in cheek. "I am very fond of chairs," explains Khun Tinakorn with only a hint of a smile, "so I am happy I could create a space to house them all! I also love colored vases in different shapes and coffee sets." This is self-evident, especially when you open the cupboards in the pristine white kitchen. Here, metal and ceramic, glass and concrete are both utilitarian — and aesthetic. A bit like the house itself, actually.

Playful shaped windows throw light from above into the double height downstairs gallery. Here, two elegant umbrella plant stems sit in a glass container on a round-topped occasional table designed by Ettore Sottsass for his Memphis Collective in the 1980s. The red chair on right is the well-known Stacking chair, designed from rigid polyurethane foam with a lacquer finish in 1960 by Verner Panton; it was the very first single-form injection-moulded plastic chair — and takes pride of place in Khun Tinakorn's collection.

Above
Reproduction of one of two chairs that Charles Rennie Mackintosh designed for Glasgow publisher Walter Blackie in 1902. Called the Hill House Ladder Back chair, it is an extremely elegant, decorative chair with slender legs and a small seat. It sits adjacent the curving staircase on the upper balcony.

Right
Large vase on left containing a pointed leaf and the taller slim model on right are both in ceramic from Seeing, a company in Bangkok. The chair is the Toy model by Philippe Starck.

Opposite
A symphony of geometry: Three leaves of variegated agave protrude from ceramic containers bought by Khun Tinakorn at Jatujak weekend market. The chair is the Miss Trip chair by Philippe Starck, so called because when fully disassembled, it fits into a small box.

Khun Tinakorn's long dining table is surrounded by some of the favorite chairs in his collection. Single stems of the golden shower orchid (oncidium) placed in bamboo are themselves placed in tall glass vases to form a regimented, yet delicate, arrangement here.

Bright colors are used to striking effect in the all-white designer kitchen.

Clockwise from top left
Award-winning fruit bowl with concealed knife from Bangkok home wares store Propaganda. Yellow gerbera in one of the owner's ceramic vases. Delicate oncidium orchid. Pink gerbera have a jaunty air in a sunshine-yellow container. Rubber picnic plates in primary colors from Assembly. Spider chrysanthemum blooms in brightly-colored glass vases from Union Victors have a retro feel.

Left
A sage-green table in a corner displays a selection of coasters, plates and glasses from Assembly. Made predominantly from rubber, they are perfect for outdoor eating.

Below
A bunch of sunflowers on the kitchen table sits behind a collection of hand-blown, colored glass wine and water glasses from Union Victors, a leading manufacturer and exporter of various glass designs in Bangkok. Cotton and linen napkins are from Jim Thompson.

A Passion for Chairs   151

Above
At one end of the ground floor a canvas by a student at the Faculty of Art and Design at Bangkok University leans against the wall behind an ergonomic white sofa called the Flying Carpet by Italian firm Cappellini. Vase, lamp, table and chairs seen previously. A bright orange silk rug from Art on the Floor helps contribute to the cheerful color scheme.

Left
A white Bubble Club armchair designed by Philippe Starck for Kartell sits next to an eggshell blue occasional table. Manufactured on an industrial scale entirely from plastic, the armchair is suitable for use both indoors and outdoors.

In general terms, Khun Tinakorn sees new design in Thailand as "a bit of a mix of styles with both Asian and Western elements." He also notes that there are more and stronger influences from Western trends, and certainly his home showcases both.

Clockwise from top left
Pale blue hydrangea blooms in a white ceramic vase. The kitschy kitchen has stainless steel utensils and bottle openers from Propaganda for colorful Bacardi breezer tipples. Assembly collection, as before. Khun Tinakorn's personal collection of coffee sets in a kitschy monchrome cabinet. Purple steel chair and gerbera. Rectangular black dinner set from Crown Ceramics and napkin from Jim Thompson; the plates also come in white if desired.

Beside a Harry Bertoia wire chair (on left) and Bubble Club armchair (center, seen previously) are two bean bags purchased from the Mae Fah Luang Foundation, a non-profit organization under Royal Patronage that was set up to help hill tribe communities in northern Thailand.

Left
The master bathroom is a mix of cool blue and white: Fittings are modern and minimal — but center stage is (naturally) reserved for the iconic S chair designed by Tom Dixon for Cappellini. The silk robe with appliqué work is by Nagara for Jim Thompson.

Left below
The downstairs cloakroom features sanitary ware from Ou Baholyodhin designed for Nahm Sanitaryware (*nahm* translates as "water") in a bulbous design that exudes a friendly feel. Scented gardenia blooms in glass containers with wrapped leaf bases are a sweet addition on the shiny vanity unit.

Overleaf
Khun Tinakorn's kitchen is all cool white with splashes of metallic hues and primary colors. A low table is often stacked with goodies, whilst a high shelf serves as a display case for his collection of aluminium coffee pots. Large elephant ears' leaves sit in a tall ceramic vase, adding a naturalistic touch.

CUSTOM-DESIGNED COMPOUND

The living/dining structure is rectangular in shape with concealed lighting and air-conditioning in the ceiling and limestone on the floors. At the far end the large panel with a gold circular motif is by Pinaree Sanpitak: entitled "The Egg" (1997) it was featured on the cover of *Art Asiapacific*, Issue 21. Sofas are set around a low-level Burmese bed that doubles up as a coffee table. The bed has a spacious storage space underneath the top level if it is opened up.

The layout of Asian houses often consists of a number of structures contained within a compound; traditionally, these would have comprised separate buildings (often open-air) to house public spaces, sleeping quarters, the kitchen and bathrooms. In more recent times, the configuration has metamorphosed into quarters for grandparents, a separate house for the children, and another smaller one for domestic utilities. This system serves the purpose of allowing family members to live together — but also gives them some privacy. It is also a pragmatic arrangement in cities where land is expensive.

In this compound in a quiet location in downtown Bangkok, five separate units are arranged in an H shape in a leafy garden. Designed by the architect Vitoon Kunalungkaran, each rectangular building is connected to its neighbor by a deck, a covered walkway or a garden path. Flat roofs, steel, glass, clean limestone and a modernist sensibility predominate. A central swimming pool, as well as a number of mature trees, offer shade and cool; it is also the heart or core of the compound.

The whole complex has a relaxed, resort-style atmosphere: This is superbly accentuated by the owner's extensive collection of Tibetan rugs and contemporary Thai art and sculpture, many of which are displayed in the main living/dining structure. Here custom-designed sliding wooden panels have been inserted the length of both sides of the gallery-sized room: these enable the owner to change artworks easily. They complement the contemporary furniture from mainly Italian designers — Minotti, lapalma, Boffi — and allow for flexibility of mood. A quick change of art can totally alter the atmosphere.

An avowed clutter-hater, the owner likes to keep the spaces clear and tidy. "The interiors are quite minimalist," she explains, "because I find that is the most relaxing décor for a home." Nonetheless, they are lively and arresting, because of the plethora of artworks, artifacts, textures and designer pieces on display. Having the luxury of space in the congested city certainly has its advantages.

View of the living/dining space as seen from the other end. The dining area in the foreground features a stark white table and leather and metal chairs, while at the far end is a double portrait of the owner by Natee Utarit.

Lighting is an important feature in this home. In addition to concealed ceiling lights, the owner displays a number of standing and hanging lamps. On far left is a bamboo-and-metal sculptural light from local artist Ping, purchased at the Jatujak Weekend Market, while on left in front of a wooden screen is a metal arc lamp.

Sliding glass doors open the family room up to the elements — with access straight on to the central swimming pool and leafy garden. Here wooden floors have replaced tiles for a warmer, more clubby feel. Two hand-fired ceramic bottles by a young Thai artist named Ping sit on a long, low table made from one piece of wood.

Above
An over-large beaten metal sculpture by local artist Jiradej Meemalai sits on a deck separating two of the living structures.

Right
The study is possibly the most cluttered room in the compound. Here one wall is entirely covered by book-cases, while another has huge windows with views of the garden.

Even though the house is clean-lined and geared towards the display of art, certain choice details prevent the rooms from becoming too much like gallery spaces. Humanizing elements are flea-market finds and personal mementoes from trips.

Clockwise from top left
Thai brass receptacles on the large bed that doubles up as a coffee table in the living room. An ironwork pouf with swathes of wool in the seating area is designed by Ping — his work features heavily in the Rayavadee Resort near Krabi. A collection of Turkish hookahs from the living room. A locally bought pot from the market is decorative in the garden.

H1 HIP

The Thonglor neighborhood has become a bit of an urban center for retro-cool shops — so H1 is well placed. Not to be missed is the Cappellini showroom featuring the latest designs of Italian furniture, Scandinavian lighting and other European home wares.

The H1 project at the end of Sukhumvit Soi 55 is a funky example of a new type of commercial complex that blurs boundaries between shopping, fashion, architecture, design, entertainment and food. Set in a series of L-shaped, glass-fronted buildings linked together by small courtyards, with a huge old tree rising from its center, it looks sleek, contemporary and welcoming.

In urban settings, where space is a premium, such places have started to replace the function of the old town square or village green. They're not just consuming centers (though you can shop, eat, drink and be entertained in them) — rather they are trendy hangouts where you can relax, meet friends and indulge in a spot of people watching. The constant interplay of space and movement, as well as the promise of retail therapy, is an enticing drama in itself.

The brainchild of a small group of young creatives, including an importer of Italian furniture, an ad exec, a fashion cum lifestyle magazine owner/photographer and a fashion designer, the complex comprises four eateries, three extravagant home furnishing shops, a bookstore and an art gallery. Each is highly individual, but all are united by the "share-share" concept. Sharing clients and courts, the boutique mall exemplifies generosity of spirit — and space.

It also gives the place an inviting air. Drop-dead design helps too, of course. Take Cappellini by Orrizonte for example: this large showroom of imported furniture sports neon shades, angular shapes, futuristic lighting and cool seating. It's got everything the average Yuppie needs to furnish an über-cool apartment. Or Hay, whose graphic, tongue-in-cheek interior is a modern interpretation of the retro ice-cream parlor. All it needs is a jukebox, and the crowds will come.

Other eateries include Extase, a Mediterranean bar and bistro, and To Die For, offering home-style French and Italian dishes. Many people's favorite, however, has to be the boho-chic Chi. Its business card bills it as "a new eclectic restaurant/lounge where one can let one's hair down, gossip and flirt all night." No wonder, really, that the complex strapline is "The New Escape on Sukhumvit."

In Cappellini, beneath
a purple hanging light, the
Supernova by Ferruccio
Laviani (2000), is a quietly
humorous black-and-white
lounging chair, the Low Pad
(1999), by British product
designer Jasper Morrison.

Right
Also in Cappellini, against a
graphic wall designed by the
owner of H1 Khun Pornsak
Rattanamethanon sit some
wonderful examples of
modern furniture: top left,
a yellow Felt Chair by Marc
Newson, top right a white
chaise longue, Orgone, also
by Marc Newson, and in the
center, two yellow Frog
chairs by Piero Lissoni.

Left
Close-ups of some of the
designs on offer, including
(on far left) a plastic chair
entitled Hole by Ronan
Bouroullec (2000).

Bright paintwork and eclectic designs characterize the interior of Chi, where lots of primary colors, graphics and shapes view for eye attention. Leaning somewhat towards a hip Japanese aesthetic, it is popular as a hang out for fashion-oriented people — models, artists and socialites, amongst others.

Above
The restaurant section of Chi at the far end features formica tabletops, leather-and-steel chairs, brightly colored floor tiles and a funky eclectic array of artifacts all around. A vase of tightly bunched pink roses in a glass vase are romantic and "girly" — totally in keeping with Chi's boudoir-chic interior.

Left
The staircase of Chi is a little like Alice in Wonderland meets Ziggy Stardust. Its bright cerise tones and zany graphics set the tone.

Colorful tiles, ribbon-bedecked mannequins, tassels and fringes, huge vases of flowers, as well as soft cushions and inviting loungers, make Chi the swanky sister of the 'hood.

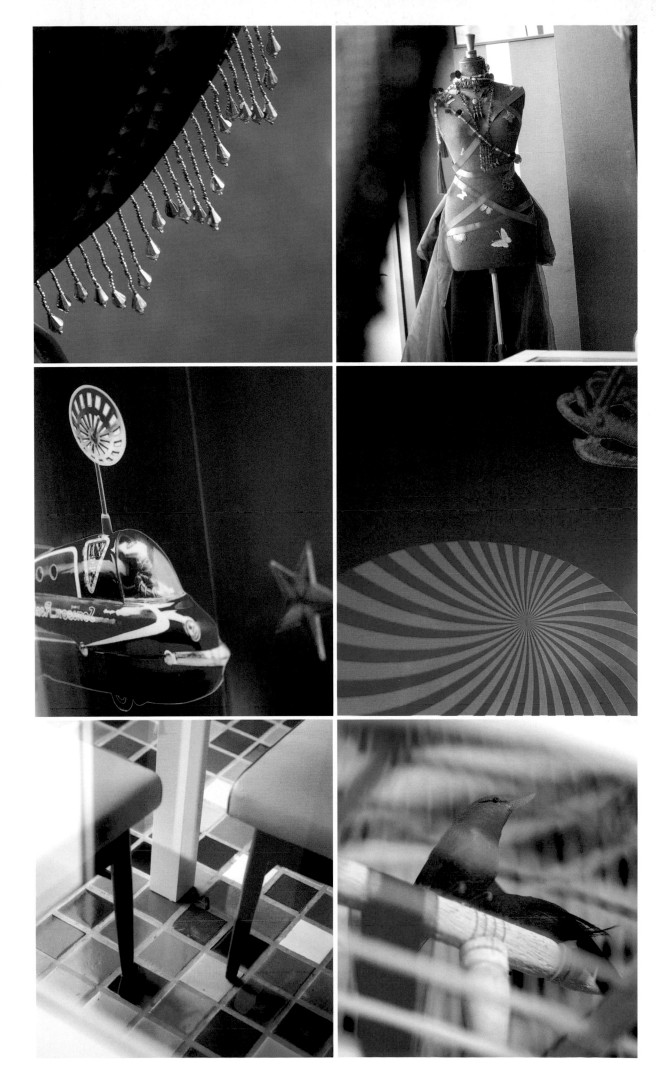

The cool interiors of ice cream parlor and café Hay were designed by Vitoon Kunalungkarn. Utilizing a palette of soft mauves and greys with a dash of orange and yellow with furniture from Cappellini, the effect is strong and geometric.

Opposite
Steel strips on the wall and ceiling were custom-designed for the ice cream parlor.

Right
"H"-shaped graphics were custom-designed in steel.

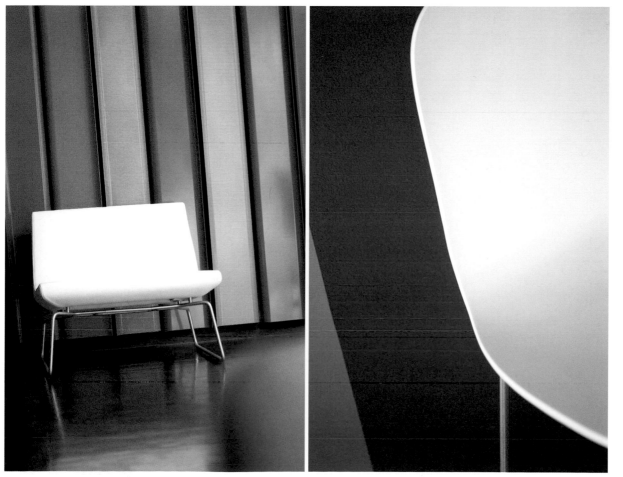

Left
Tate chair (2003) by Jasper Morrison, a stackable chair with stainless steel legs and lacquered seat. Morrison was commissioned by the Tate Modern in London's Southbank to design much of the furniture for the gallery; this chair takes its name from that project.

Far left
Superlight white 2-seater sofa by Barber & Osgerby (2000).

Geo Décor is owned by three partners — an owner of a women's magazine who is a well-known photographer and experienced gardener, a fashion designer and a business woman. The decor is influenced by French design — with red wood, European crystal chandeliers and a cozy, yet clean, look.

Far left
The photographer owner takes arty shots, and transforms them into wonderful gifts. Here a cool cabinet displays notebooks and wrapping paper in a variety of designs.

Left
Postcards are picture postcard pretty.

Below
With fashion items upstairs, and gifts below, this section of the shop sells gardening tools, plants, water features and wrought-iron garden furniture.

WHITE & LIGHT

The open-plan living room is a mix of modern and antique. Contemporary Italian pieces, white walls, teak floors and a collection of antique Buddhas give the room a soothing feeling.

This downtown duplex apartment is a convincing illustration of the importance of fine lighting. Almost totally open-plan, the home of Troy Schooneman and Surachet Timsakul has two sources of light. The first comes from the enormous windows that afford almost 360 degree views over the city; the second is the result of a professionally designed system that allows for great flexibility. Formulated by Palicon with state-of-the-art equipment from Europe, it enables the owners to create different moods, brightnesses and colors depending on the occasion.

"If we are having a party, we can turn our apartment into a bar," enthuses Khun Surachet, "But if we just want to relax after a hard day's work, we put on the dimmer, go for a soft shade — and chill."

That, plus an absence of clutter, is the key to this clean-lined space. Originally eight small units on two floors, an imaginative conversion has resulted in one huge open-plan space downstairs with an open staircase accessing two bedrooms, bathroom and library/office above. Concealed cupboards, large pivoting doors and cleverly crafted storage units help to keep mess to a minimum.

With a total of 540 square meters (5,800 sq ft) of floor space, the apartment is large by any standards. Teak wood flooring acts as a warming contrast to white walls, and tactile furnishings and rugs further soften hard edges. Furniture is mainly modern Italian, and mostly in dark shades — contributing to the general monochromatic theme. The owners venerate the Buddha, so have a wonderful collection of Buddha statues — both to pay homage to and to add a sense of history to the apartment. "We didn't want the apartment to be too modern," explains Khun Surachet. "We don't like clinical modern, so we use the softness of the Buddha and some antique pieces to cut down [a] too modern feeling."

The owners love white and light and don't want to see the minutiae of daily life when they get home after work. "We love our space," they say. "We want our home to be clear at all times." However, everything may not be as it first appears: If you open a door, you're more likely to be confronted with shelves of books or a deep cupboard, than another room. It's all part of the clever design.

Left
The upper floor landing bathed in white light doesn't have even a hint of clutter.

Opposite
An impressive stainless steel and wood staircase leads up to the private quarters. Situated almost centrally, it is a sculptural feature in itself. Beneath it and through, one can see the large black dining table from Poliform decorated with an informal arrangement of hydrangeas and river pebbles in tall glasses.

Below
The apartment is perfect for entertaining: Central to comfort in the living area is a configuration of KlinE sofas by Rodolfo Dordoni for Minotti — deep and satisfying, the form can be changed into different permutations if so wished. Behind is the dining area and an adjacent open-plan Arclinea kitchen.

Deep purple: Large pivoting glass-and-steel doors lead from the large terrace into the open plan space on the ground floor. Having lived previously in a cluttered space with lots of antiques, the owners decided a total change was in order. Their present home (seen here bathed in soothing purple light) is the antithesis of their previous one — spacious, clean and clear, it gives them an environment in which to breathe and relax.

Above
The upstairs landing leading
to the private quarters:
At the far end is an antique
Khmer statue, one of a
pair of Hindu gods and god-
desses, Vissanu and Uma.

Left
Concealed storage behind
frosted glass door that has
a dual function: it is either a
door or a cupboard door.

Far left
Every area in this apartment
is light-filled. Looking down
the staircase to doors leading on to the huge deck,
you get a feeling of almost
floating above the city. As
the apartment is on the 18th
and 19th floors of a centrally
located condo, the views are
far-reaching and dramatic,
particularly at night.

LAID-BACK LIVING

Right
Evenings at the house on peaceful Paknampran Beach are idyllic: once doors are flung open and music and barefoot guests drift in and out, the house takes on an easy, outdoorsy vibe.

Below
Illumination on the rooftop deck comes from black ceramic candle holders by Gilles Caffier, a French interior designer based in Asia. His products — ranging from candle holders to trays, dishes and the like — have super fine detailing and high quality, and are exported all over the world.

Designed by Kanika Ratanapridakul, the young Thai architect probably best known for her contribution to China's Great Wall Commune project, this beach house is a celebration of the synthesis of nature and architecture. Proving that strong, rectilinear forms are not at odds with sand-dunes, casuarinas trees and scrub, the house is a sexy mixture of voids and planes both indoor and outdoor, using modern materials and a very contemporary style.

Commissioned by Bangkok residents Punnee Chaiyakul and Hans Willems as a weekend retreat, the house is divided into two sections: one side houses the guest wing, the other the main wing. Both sections have extensive roof terracing and open decks between as well as fronting the sea. Interestingly enough, its form is an adaptation of the layout of the traditional Thai house that had closed living quarters on two sides and an open *chan-ban* platform in the middle.

Walls, and often floors, are predominantly polished cement rendering on brick, while Malaysian *teng* wood is used for decking and dividing screens. Enormous floor-to-ceiling glass windows invite in light and sea views. Even though the house may look a little imposing from outside, the little arboretum within which it stands and the gorgeous beach setting considerably soften the architectural starkness. Paraphrasing one of William McDonough's Hannover Principles, laid down as a guide to sustainable design, the architect notes: "I wanted to treat nature as a model and a mentor, not as an inconvenience to be evaded or controlled."

Certainly, the open-to-the-elements, well ventilated layout is the property's greatest strength. "When we visit," says Hans, "we feel ourselves in the fresh air, with the beautiful birds, pines, sea and beach around us. Even if we sit inside (usually we sit on the deck), we are in the midst of this wonderful nature: we become part of it."

In keeping with the laid back atmosphere, furniture is simple and often made from wood. Ironically, however, the crème de la crème of relaxing spots is to be found on the furniture-free rooftop terrace: here wood from the deck can be raised to form impromptu loungers — and with candles lit, the sounds of the waves on the shore and a panorama of stars above, you won't want to leave.

Right

The living room features two ash wood circular rockers by Existenze and custom-designed sofa, as well as extensive French doors leading out to the beach. A *teng* wood slatted screen separates the room from the music room behind. On the split level dark wood coffee table from China Group sits a casual, organic betel nut palm fruit arrangement in a Gilles Caffier black ceramic bowl.

Below

The white oak trestle type dining table and benches from China Group, a furniture/interiors contracting company, are perfect for summer picnic meals. Young coconut flowers plucked from a tree are displayed on a square wooden tray from Asian Motif.

Above
A view out to sea. When sourcing furniture for the house, Hans explains: "We tried to keep away from heavy furniture, so we chose more light and airy items in keeping with the house."

Left
Enormously heavy ceramic pot designed by Studio of the North, an award-winning ceramic company in Lampang. This vessel illustrates a fine combination of contemporary shapes and forms together with traditional glazing techniques — a hallmark of founders Grittip Sirirattumrong and Atchara Tejapaibul's work.

Opposite
The house's uncompromising exterior seen during the day.

On the front terrace are two striking wooden chairs and a table by Bangkok furniture design company Existenze; looking out to sea they are a modern take on the traditional deck chair.

Above
A custom-made bed with satin embroidered cushions by Ploenchan Vinyaratn Pornsurat from Beyond Living sits in front of a wooden screen in the ground-floor guest bedroom. The unusual chair, called the S-Lounge Chair, is in dark-stained teak wood and comes from China Group.

Left
Bathrooms are a combination of the indoors and the outdoors with extensive use of wood, polished concrete and glass. Young coconut flowers in a black stone vase from Gilles Caffier on a monumental washstand are fresh, minimal and outdoorsy in the master bathroom.

Right
Outdoor shower for tropical bathing.

Far right
Papillons (Butterflies) is the name given to this line of hand-produced cushions from Beyond Living.

STRONG GEOMETRY, GOOD QI

This house is a sterling example of how a seamless integration between indoors and outdoors may be achieved within a thoroughly modern architectural milieu. Built in a u-shape around a central courtyard in a family compound, the owners were very specific about their needs. "We wanted a continuous flow of space, natural light and ventilation, as well as a flow of vision and function between interior and exterior spaces," says owner Khun Korakot Srivikorn. As her husband Khun Predapond Bandityanond is the managing director of Landscape Architect 49 Ltd, he worked closely with architect Duangrit Bunnag to meet the brief.

Bunnag, well known both as the editor of architectural magazine art4d and as the architect of Costa Lanta, a resort in Southern Thailand, as well as a number of private homes in Bangkok, is a friend of the owners. His work, he asserts, combines modern forms and materials for the most part culled from the West with a Thai sensibility and respect for culture and climate. Much of his work is of a pared-down, sheared nature; by removing superfluities, he reduces a structure to its essential core.

Geometric lines, an all-white palette, voluminous rooms and floor-to-ceiling doors and windows predominate. Using prefabricated concrete that is plastered and painted, as well as glass, wood and aluminum, the three-story house is imposing and attractive. A limestone courtyard and lawn, black granite goldfish pond, tall glass-and-aluminum pivoting doors, an open-to-the-sky entrance forecourt, hedges to define outdoor spaces and overhangs all contribute to the connection of the interior within its setting.

The house appeals because of its apparent simplicity. Clutter- and frill-free, storage spaces are either hidden or built into walls. Cool, white, urban, hip (but never cold), it is representative of a new wave of Thai architecture. Its owners feel it has good *qi* (energy) and they like living in harmony with the "natural light, trees, birds, squirrels, even frogs in season." And since they have a more "English-style garden house" in the country outside Chiang Mai, this metropolitan home acts is its perfect foil. It's called having the best of both worlds.

The house is as impressive
for its details as for its overall architecture: Here, wood,
white and steel are strongly
minimal.

Opposite
View from the staircase into
the courtyard. Imported
white limestone continues
from the outside into the
ground floor, ensuring continuity from outside to in.

Overleaf
In the vast dining room, a
Duangrit Bunnag-designed
oversized table with recessed
legs is a composite of different kinds of wood such
as teak and white oak. Simple
Italian brown leather chairs
keep the focus on the table.
A bright yellow chrysanthemum arrangement thereon
exudes warmth and wel-
come. To achieve the round-
ed shape Khun Sakul carved
the oasis into a dome — and
white ceramic containers
offset it perfectly. On a table
in the background on right,
are five quirky hand crafted
containers by artist Thaiwijit
Puengkasemsomboon plant-
ed with euphorbias; behind
and outside are planter
boxes attached to a severe
white wall.

Above left
Rock-a-bye bench by artist turned furniture designer Paiwate Wangbon from Craft Factor.

Above right
A collection of antique walking sticks from India is displayed at the bottom of the stairs.

Opposite
A large landing upstairs is a good lounging spot, with views out on to the garden. On right is a red Infinity armchair by Paiwate Wangbon and on left is a black cowhide Foglia chaise lounge by Korpan Leopairote, both from Craft Factor.

Overlooking the goldfish
pond, huge windows give
garden vistas from the living
room. Modular furniture
from Minotti at Orizzonte in
shades of pale grey is
accessorized with mauve,
pink and rust scatter
cushions from Cocoon.
The overall effect is calm,
balanced and civilized.

Above
The top floor houses the bedrooms and an orchid nursery, pictured here. Two eye-catching chairs designed by Nuttapong C. at Sculpture, a shop that specializes in the avant-garde, are part of a collection that is exported to Canada, France, Germany, Russia, Turkey and Hong Kong. On left is the yellow SEXY dining chair in wood with a metal frame and cotton strap, on right the orange SWAY wood and metal chair with cotton strap.

Left
The geometric forms of modern and custom-crafted furniture work well in a house where right angles predominate.

Textures, details and forms are all "just-so" in this near perfect house.

Clockwise from top left
Stainless steel banisters on the staircase; euphorbia plants; curved backrest on the Infinity armchair; hand-fired ceramic bowls from the Studio of the North; close-up of the detailing on the SWAY chair; goldfish in the black granite pond.

ACKNOWLEDGMENTS

We would like to thank the following for their invaluable help during the production of this book:

M.L. Chiratorn Chirapravati, Ms Atchara Tejapaibul, Mr Bhasan Itdhikul, Mr Chatchawan Pisitpaisankun, Ms Jantana Sawaengkit, Mr Kitti Chaithiraphant, Mr Kittipong Wangsuwannasri, Ms Marika Charoenkitivarakorn, Ms Minako Ooka, Mr Nagara Sambandaraksa, Ms Nathima Indrapana, Ms Nicharee Thongprapai, Ms Nijaya Intaraprasong, Mr Nuttapong Charoenkitivarakorn, Mr Ou Baholyodhin, Mr Panarin Manuyakorn, Ms Panitaka Srikuttanaprom, Ms Ploenchan Mook Phornsurat, Ms Pradthana Jotikasthira, Ms Rabeab Meesapanant, Ms Rocky Hizon, Ms Rose Chalalai Singh, Ms Rungsima Kasikranund, Mr Scott Whittaker, Ms Sivika Karnasuta, Ms Supawinee Rungsawat, Ms Tam Devakul, Mrs Theeranuj Karnasuta, Mr Varanon Ketkaroonkul and Mr Wichakom Topungtiem.

Properties

Surachet Timsakul and Troy Schooneman, Rika Dila, Vichien Chansevikul and Michael Palmer, Jean Michel Beurdeley and Patsri Bunnag, Punjavadee Tanvilai and Pichet Puengpa, Kritsada and Amparin Tanvilai, Yvan Van Outrive and Wongvipa Devahastin na Ayudhya, Korakot Srivikorn and Predapond Bandidyanont, Prabhakorn Vadanyakul and Dr Yuvanuch Kiatiwongse, Wisit Jivakul, Punnee Chaiyakul and Hans Willems, Tinakorn Rujinarong, Ek-Anong Phanachet and Carlos Manalae, Arthur Napolitano, Masa and Michael Unsworth, Somchai Piraban and Brian Renaud, Prakit Woraprasit, Pornsak Rattanamethanon, Sanya Souvanna Phouma.

Suppliers

Able Interior Workshop Co. Ltd.
41/7 Soi Rama 2(69), Rama 2 Rd.
Bankhuntien, Bangkok 10150.
tel: (662) 892 8606/8414, fax: 892 8415
email: ableinter@yahoo.com

Art on the Floor
2/4 The Promenade D cor, Nai Lert Hotel
Bangkok, 2nd floor room 26, Wireless Road,
Bangkok 10330.
tel: (662) 655 4249/50, fax: 655 4250
email: ning@carpetmaker.co.th

Ayodhya Ltd. partnership
1028/5 Rama 5 Road, Thungmahamek,
Sathorn, Bangkok 10120.
tel: (662) 679 8521, fax: 679 8522
email: info@ayodhyatrade.com
www.ayodhyatrade.com

beyond living Co. Ltd
23 Sorachai Building, 18th Floor
Soi Sukhumvit 63, North Klongton,
Wattana, Bangkok 10110.
tel: (662) 714 3109/10, fax: 382 1976
email: marketing@beyond-living.com
www.beyond-living.com

China Group Co. Ltd
1268-72 Soi Charoensuk Sukhumvit Road,
Klongtoey, Bangkok.
tel: (662) 258 3214/9850, fax: 259 4141
email: info@cgfurniture.com
www.cgfurniture.com

Christian Liaigre
HYLE, 2/4, Nai Lert Tower, 2nd Floor, Suite
36 Wireless Road, Lumpini, Pathumwan
Bangkok 10330.
tel: (662) 655 0388, fax: 655 2483
email: sales@christian-liaigre.co.th

Cocoon Design Co. Ltd
999 Gaysorn Plaza, 3rd Floor, Room 3-03,
3-04 Ploenchit Road, Limpini, Pathumwan,
Bangkok 10330.
tel: (662) 656 1006, fax: 656 1007
email: cocoon@asianet.co.th

Craft Factor Co. Ltd
Yada Building, 4th Floor, Room 4/10,
56 Silom Road, Bangrak, Bangkok 10500.
tel: (662) 632 8771, fax: 632 8772
email: customerservice@crafactor.com
www.crafactor.com

Crown Ceramics Co. Ltd
Ceratex Bldg. 54/456 Moo 5 Pattanakarn
Road, Pravej, Bangkok 10250.
tel: (662) 721 6599, fax: 721 6533
email: office@crownceramics.com
www.crownceramics.com

E.G.G. Enterprise Co. Ltd
19 Rama 9 Road, Suanluang,
Bangkok 10250.
tel: (662) 300 5131/4, fax: 300 5559
email: decor@eggthai.com
www.eggthai.com

Gilles Caffier
Siam Discovery Center, 4th Floor, Unit No:
410 Rama 1, Pathumwan, Bangkok 10330.
tel: (662) 658 0487, fax: 934 5647
email: commercial@gillescaffier.com
www.gillescaffier.com

Jim Thompson
9 Suriwongse Road, Bangkok 10500.
tel: (662) 632 8100, fax: 236 6777 / 237 1018
email: office@jimthompson.com
www.jimthompson.com

Juku
611/17 Charoenkrung Road, Bangkloe,
Bangkorlaem, Bangkok 10120.
tel: (662) 678 9059/289 0998, fax: 287 3960
email: juku@loxinfo.co.th
www.juku.com

Leatherparagon (2000) Co. Ltd.
99/18-19 Soi Budda-Osote, Siphya Bangrak,
Bangkok 10500.
tel: (662) 233 4182/234 1912, fax: 266 5957
email: vichen@leatherparagon.com
www.leatherparagon.com

Lotus Arts de Vivre
Showrooms at Four Seasons, The Oriental,
The Peninsula, The Sukhothai, Bangkok and
Amanpuri, Phuket.
tel: (662) 250 0732, fax: 250 0730
em: customerservice@lotusartsdevivre.com
www.lotusartsdevivre.com

Niwat
Gaysorn Plaza, 3rd Floor,
No.3F-20 999 Ploenchit Road, Lumpini,
Pathumwan, Bangkok 10330.
tel: (662) 656 1081, fax: 656 1073
email: niwat@nv-aranyik.com
www.aranyik.thaiexponet.com

Panta
Siam Discovery Center 4th Floor, Unit No:
411-2 Rama 1, Pathumwan, Bangkok 10330.
tel: (662) 658 0415, fax: 658 0417
email: panta1@loxinfo.co.th

Planet (2001) Co. Ltd
1028/5 Rama 5 Road, Thungmahamek,
Sathorn, Bangkok 10120.
tel: (662) 679 8525, fax: 679 8524
email: info@planet2001design.com
www.planet2001design.com

Rapeeleela
8 Racquet Club, Sukhumvit 49/9 Klongton-
naur, Wattana, Bangkok 10110.
tel: (662) 712 8044, fax: 712 8030
email: rapee@rapeeleela.net
www.rapeeleela.net

The Studio of the North
52/3 Phaholyothin Soi 7, Phaholyothin Road,
Phayathai, Bangkok 10400.
tel: (662) 619 5923, fax: 619 5923
email: atcharatejapaibul@hotmail.com

Sculpture
43/156 Moo 5, Kanjanapisek Road,
Bangbon, Bangkok 10150.
tel: (662) 895 0739/454 4957, fax: 895 0739
email: nuttapong@hotmail.com
www.thesculpture.net

T Positif Shop
The Peninsula Plaza 2nd Floor, Room 210,
153 Radamri Road Bangkok 10330.
tel: (662) 652 2184, fax: 652 2184
email: info@tpositif.com
www.tpositif.com

Union Victors Co. Ltd
161 Yawapanich Road, Songwad,
Bangkok 10100.
tel: (662) 222 9993/9989, 221 4251
fax: 225 6007/0424
email: uvglas@loxinfo.co.th
www.unionvictor.com

Yothaka Int'l Co. Ltd
1028/5 Rama 4 Road, Thungmahamek
Sathorn, Bangkok 10120.
tel: (662) 679 8628/31/32, fax: 679 8965
email: yathaka@cscoms.com
www.yathaka.thailand.com

Commercial

Bed Supperclub
26 Soi Sukhumvit 11, Sukhumvit Rd.
Klongtoey-nua, Wattana, Bangkok 10110.
tel: (662) 651 3537, fax: 651 3538
email: info@bedsupperclub.com
www.bedsupperclub.com

Budji Living
Soi Sang-Ngern (Thonglor 25),
Sukhumvit Road, Klongton-nua, Wattana,
Bangkok 10110.
tel: (662) 712 9833, fax: 712 9834
email: bliving@budjibangkok.com

H1
998 Sukhumvit, 55 Thonglor, Klongton-nua,
Wattana, Bangkok 10110.

– Basheer Design Books (Thai) Ltd.
H1, 988/7 Sukhumvit 55 Thonglor, Klongton-
nua, Wattana, Bangkok 10110.
tel: (662) 391 9815/6, fax: 391 9814
email:basheerthailand@basheergraphic.com
www.basheergraphic.com

– Cappellini Showrom
H1, 998 Sukhumvit 55 Thonglor, Klongton-
nua, Wattana, Bangkok 10110.
tel: (662) 391 9101, fax: 714 7800
email: orizzonteco@yahoo.com

– Chi
H1, 998/5 Sukhumvit 55 Thonglor, Klongton-
nua, Wattana, Bangkok 10110.
tel: (662) 381 7587/9, fax: 381 7585

– Extase
H1, 998/2 Sukhumvit 55 Thonglor, Klongton-
nua, Wattana, Bangkok 10110.
tel: (662) 381 4322/3, fax: 381 4323
email: g_management1997@yahoo.com

– Geo Decor Co. Ltd
H1, 998/6 Sukhumvit 55 Thonglor, Klongton-
nua, Wattana, Bangkok 10110.
tel: (662) 381 4324, fax: 381 4325
email: geo@ego.co.th
www.geo.co.th

– Hay
H1, 998/3 Sukhumvit 55 Thonglor, Klongton-
nua, Wattana, Bangkok 10110.
tel: (662) 391 7577, fax: 391 9104

– To Die For
H1, 998 Sukhumvit 55 Thonglor, Klongton-
nua, Wattana, Bangkok 10110.
tel: (662) 381 4714, fax: 381 4715
email: manager@stardog.co.th

Hutchison CAT Wireless Multimedia Ltd
1768 IFCT Tower, 23rd Floor,
New Pechburi Road, Bangkapi,
Huaykwang, Bangkok 10320.
tel: (662) 288 8822
email: contact@hutch.co.th
www.hutch.co.th

Kudu Company Ltd. (The Lofts Sathorn)
Room 156, The Millennia Bldg.
62 Soi Langsuan, Bangkok 10330.
tel: (662) 651 9669, fax: 651 9943
email: info@kuduthailand.com
www.kuduthailand.com

Le Motif Co., Ltd.
171/59 Ladprao 80, Wangthonglang,
Bangkok 10310.
tel: (662) 932 7227, fax: 932 7277
email: info@lemotif.com
www.lemotif.com

Sirocco
63rd Floor, State Tower Bangkok., 1055
Silom Road, Bangrak, Bangkok 10500.
tel: (662) 624 9555, fax: 624 9554
www.thedomebkk.com

100 Tonson Gallery
100 Soi Tonson, Ploenchit Rd., Lumpini,
Pathumwan, Bangkok 10330.
tel: (662) 652 1191, fax: 652 1191
email: info@100tonsongallery.com
www.100tonsongallery.com

Vihayas
Gaysorn Plaza, Unit 21-6 & 21-7, 3rd Floor,
999 Ploenchit Road, Lumpini, Pathumwan,
Bangkok 10330.
tel: (662) 656 1790, fax: 656 1798
email: info@vihayas.co.th
www.vihayas.co.th

Architects

Attayut Piravinich
I.A.W. Limited
77/19 Soi Ekamai,
21 Sukhumvit 63 Road,
Wattana, Bangkok 10110.
tel: (662) 711 6477-8, fax: 711 6463
email: iawbkk@asiaaccess.net.th

Duangrit Bunnag
Duangrit Bunnag Architect Limited
989 28th Floor, Unit B3,
Siam Tower, Rama I Road,
Pathumwan, Bangkok 10330.
tel: (662) 658 0580-1, fax: 658 0582
email: duangrit@loxinfo.co.th

Kanika Ratanapridakul
Spacetime Architects
4th Floor, 32 Soi Soonvijai 8 [3],
Petchburi Road, Bangkapi, Huaykwang,
Bangkok 10320.
tel: (662) 718 1533-35, fax: 318 7717
email: admin@spacetime.co.th

Ou Baholyodhin
Ou Baholyodhin Studio
Unit 2C 9-15, Elthorne Road,
London N19 4AJ, UK.

Mr Panarin Manuyakorn
G.I.M Design Studio Co., Ltd.
89/27-28 Villa 49, Sukhumvit 49 North,
Klongton, Wattana, Bangkok 10110.
tel: (662) 712 9484-5, fax: 392 0994
email: info@gimdesign.com
www.gimdesign.com

Prabhakorn Vadanyakul
Architects 49 Ltd.
81 Soi Sukhumvit 26, Kongton,
Klongtoey, Bangkok 10110.
tel: (662) 259 4370, fax: 260 4370
email: a49@a49.com
www.a49.com

Scott Whittaker
dwp cityspace ltd.
The Dusit Thani Building, Penthouse level
11, 946 Rama IV Road, Bangkok 10500.
tel: (662) 267 3939, fax: 267 3949
email: thailand@dwpartnership.com
dwpartnership@com

Tinakorn Rujinarong
Joe & Tinakorn
21/45 Soi Jomphon Ladprao 15,
Jatujak, Bangkok 10900.
tel: (662) 938 8029, fax: 513 2144